CHESS
A BEGINNER'S GUIDE

1. Two highly ornamental chess pieces from the collection of Mr. Frank Greygoose. *Left*. A Chinese ivory queen of about 1800. *Right*. An Indian ivory queen of about 1800 which has been colourfully treated by staining and lacquering.

CHESS
A BEGINNER'S GUIDE

by

STANLEY MORRISON

LONDON
LUTTERWORTH PRESS

First published 1968

7188   1365   0

*Printed in Great Britain at
the Pitman Press
Bath*

ACKNOWLEDGEMENTS

THE author would like to acknowledge his considerable indebtedness to: his colleague, Mr. R. Bott, for advice he has offered throughout the various stages in the preparation of this book; Mr. A. J. McMinn for advice given at the manuscript stage; Mr. A. Reilly, Technical Editor of the *British Chess Magazine*, for advice on general matters concerned with production; Mr. R. G. Wade, whose research into the thinking processes which go into the calculation of chess moves, prompted the chapter on Move Drill, page 118.

The Frontispiece is reproduced by permission of the Chelsea Antiques Fair, the illustration of the Lewis chess pieces in Plate 2 by the Trustees of the British Museum, and the Pepys chess pieces (also shown in Plate 2) by permission of the London Museum. The illustrations in Plates 3, 4, 5 and 6 were supplied by Mr. A. Reilly and Plate 7 by Paul Popper, Ltd.

CONTENTS

CONTENTS

LIST OF PLATES

INTRODUCTION

THE first known book of chess rules was written by a Spaniard named Lucena, in about 1497, although the game was by then already hundreds of years old. The game of chess, played on a chequered board between two opponents who play alternately, one move at a time, is the oldest—and best—board game in the world!

The terms such as 'End Game', 'Middle Game', 'Opening', etc., which you will find in this book, reflect the stages through which games of chess progress. Although it is rarely possible to determine exactly where one stage ends and another begins, such categories are useful not only for purposes of identification but also for facilitating the logical step-by-step approach to the various aspects of the game by the student.

Do not, in the early stages of your chess apprenticeship, worry unduly about an exact understanding and use of appropriate terminology. Although a correct appreciation of chess terms is an undoubted advantage, it is more important, by far, to concentrate on the play rather than the words. Master the fundamental principles first, and let the correct use of chess vocabulary follow. Avoid learning off by heart series of moves copied from experts, unless you are able to justify them, for you will not win many games if you make a habit of playing moves for which you cannot see the need!

Some of the diagrams in the text have been designed to show only a part of the chessboard and only those pieces (chessmen) which are relevant to the matter being discussed. This has been done to highlight the points being made. Pieces and parts of the board omitted in this way should be regarded as having no bearing on the examples being illustrated.

From time to time, advice is given concerning practice exercises, and tests have been set to enable you to check your understanding of the principles dealt with. It is recommended that you set up the various instructive, practice and test positions and *play them over across the chessboard*. Full advantage will be gained from the practice exercises only if you carry them out in the presence of another player, for since these exercises will have been worked out by the reader, no answers, or checks upon their validity, will be found in the book. In answering test questions which require that individual squares or lines of squares be indicated, the use of tracing paper may be found helpful in ensuring that the pages of the book are not marked.

Unless otherwise directed, you should attempt the test questions without reference to other parts of the book for help! Beneath the solutions are given references to pages where the information relevant to the questions set may be found. In certain cases it is recommended that incorrectly interpreted questions be reconsidered before proceeding to the next stage. In other cases, where it is considered that understanding is likely to be reinforced in succeeding pages, doubtful interpretations may safely be left for subsequent reconsideration.

At the end of the book will be found a pull-out reference page showing, at a glance, important geographical aspects of the chessboard.

CHAPTER 1

THE CHESSBOARD

A Chequered Battlefield

H ERE it is. Eight rows of eight squares. There must always be a white square in the bottom right hand corner.

I

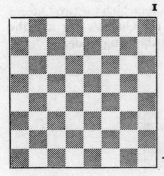

← white square bottom right.

There are many straight lines of squares on a chessboard, some running from left to right, some from the nearside to the farside and some diagonally.

Diagram 2 shows the pieces in their correct positions at the start of the game, with recognised symbols to represent the chessmen.

It is usual in chess books to arrange the diagrams so that the white pieces move up from the bottom and the black pieces move down from the top. All the diagrams in this book are arranged in this way.

Board right way round? White square bottom right!

13

2

Knight Queen Bishop Rook
Rook Bishop King Knight

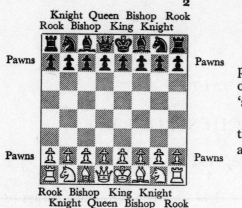

Pawns   Pawns

Pawns   Pawns

Rook Bishop King Knight
Knight Queen Bishop Rook

The squares on which the pieces stand at the beginning of a game are known as the 'starting' squares.

There may not be more than one piece on a square at any time.

You will notice in Diagram 3 below that a dividing line has been drawn down the centre of the board. The half on which the two Queens stand at the start of the game is known as the Queen's side and the other half, on which the two Kings stand, as the King's side.

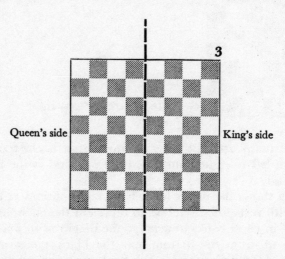

3

Queen's side   King's side

Each side commences with a force of sixteen pieces of six different kinds, King, Queen, two Rooks, two Bishops, two Knights and eight

2. Probably invented in India before the seventh century, chess is one of the oldest games in the world. The walrus ivory chessmen shown *above* are thought to have been made in Scandinavia about the middle of the twelfth century, and were discovered at Uig on the Isle of Lewis in 1831. The illustration *below* is of a seventeenth-century chessboard and a selection of pieces, which form part of the set presented to Samuel Pepys by James II.

Pawns. In all games, players move alternately, making one move at a time. White moves first.

It is a rule in chess that if you touch one of your pieces you must move it, if it is your turn to move, unless it is illegal to do so. Similarly, if you touch one of your opponent's pieces you must capture it, unless such a move would be against the rules. Should you wish to adjust a piece which has been dislodged on its square, you may do so, provided you first warn your opponent of your intention. A common warning used on such occasions is the French expression *j'adoube*, which means 'I adjust', but any reasonable warning remark will suffice. If it is your turn to move and you adjust a piece on its square without giving such a warning, your opponent may insist that you make a move with the piece which has been touched. (No penalty is exacted if you touch a piece without giving warning, *if it is your opponent's turn to move*.)

In the course of most battles on the chessboard, forces become mobilised for action, movements of attack and defence take place and captures are made. For the course of each game you will become, as it were, the General in charge of an army, pitting not only your forces but also your wits, against those of your adversary. If your skill and that of your opponent are roughly equal, then you will have an exciting battle; if your opponent has the advantage over you of superior skill, then you will have the counter advantage of learning from his greater ability—and your own mistakes! There is always pleasure and sometimes more than a little glory in winning a game of chess, and yet the considerable consolation of being able to benefit from your shortcomings should make your losses less hard to bear. It is for this reason that you should play as often as possible against opponents whose skill exceeds your own.

To gain the maximum advantage from this book you are advised to set up the various puzzles, positions and games and play the moves over on a chessboard!

Although it sometimes happens that a player gives up (resigns) during a game when further resistance would be of no avail, the object of the game is . . .

the capture of your opponent's King—checkmate!

15

The Lines of Movement on the Chessboard

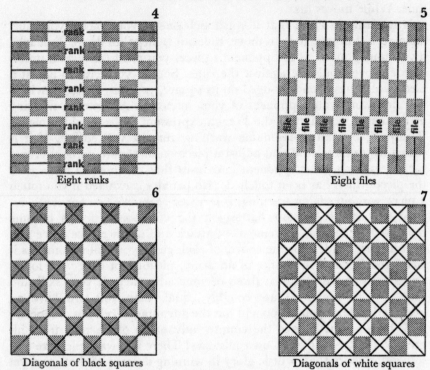

4

Eight ranks

5

Eight files

6

Diagonals of black squares

7

Diagonals of white squares

Unlike ranks and files, all of which are eight squares long, the diagonals vary in length from two to eight squares. Since the diagonal of a square is longer than the length of its side, a given number of consecutive squares along a diagonal is longer than the same number of squares along rank or file, when considered from the point of view of linear measure. In chess, however, we count distance in squares. For example, the distance from the black square in the bottom left hand corner of the chessboard to the other end of the file on the one hand, and the distance from the same starting square to the black square at the other end of the long diagonal on the other, is the same when counted in squares, despite the fact that the diagonal journey may appear to be longer. The rows of squares in these diagrams are vital lines of communications along which the forces will engage each other.

Eight ranks, eight files and 26 diagonals on every chessboard!

Practice

Learn to set up the pieces on their starting squares. Start as follows, without referring to other parts of the book. First ensure that the board is the right way round—white square bottom right. Then, assuming you are White, put a white Queen on a white square, on the rank nearest you, with the King on the adjoining square of the same rank, so that both pieces occupy the two centre squares. Now place a Rook (formerly known as 'castle') on each end square of the same rank. Since we associate castles with knights in shining armour, put a Knight next to each Rook and then with Bishops occupying the two remaining vacant squares on the rank, all that remains is to place a white Pawn in front of each piece and White is ready. Set up the black pieces in the same way, at the other end of the board, and battle may be joined. Make the Queen (white Queen on a white square, black Queen on a black square) your starting point in setting up the board, until your proficiency makes such a guide unnecessary.

2

HOW TO LABEL THE SQUARES

THE ability to keep a record of chess moves ('chess notation') is a useful aid in improving your standard of play, for not only does it permit mistakes to be examined but techniques of stronger players to be studied. Chess notation allows games of chess played centuries ago, to be re-lived and enjoyed time and time again. Who knows, perhaps *you*, in the not too distant future, may present posterity with a brilliancy which will find its way in some collection of 'greats'. Anyway, make a start by finding out how the squares are labelled!

The following are the letters used to represent the various pieces. You will notice that in order to differentiate between the pairs of Rooks, Bishops and Knights on each side of the board, the letter 'Q' precedes the Rooks, Bishops and Knights on the Queen's side, whilst 'K' precedes their partners on the King's side:

K	King	Q	Queen
KR	King's Rook	QR	Queen's Rook
KB	King's Bishop	QB	Queen's Bishop
KKt	King's Knight	QKt	Queen's Knight

Pawns are represented by the initial letters of the piece which stands behind them on the starting squares, followed by the letter 'P'. The Pawn which, at the start of the game, stands in front of the Queen's Rook is QRP, that on the Queen's Bishop's file QBP, and so on. It should be noted that, except in the case of Pawns, these identities do not change although, in the course of the game, many of the pieces will move away from the lines on which they started. The special problem of Pawn identification will be dealt with later.

Now let us begin by labelling the squares from the point of view of the player with the white pieces. Give to all the squares of each file the initial letters of the piece on the starting square of the file concerned. Add to the letters of squares of the rank nearest to you (the first rank), the number '1', add number '2' to the letters of the squares of the next rank (second rank), '3' to the letters of the squares of the third rank, and so on, until you reach number '8' for the squares of the eighth rank. You will now have each square labelled with a combination of file letters and rank numbers. Similarly, Black's first rank is the one nearest to him. Black's squares may now be labelled, using '1' for *Black's* first rank labels, '2' for his second rank labels, and so on, up to '8'.

Diagram 8 shows the squares labelled from the point of view of the player with the white pieces, and Diagram 9 shows the squares labelled for the black pieces:

8

QR8	QKt8	QB8	Q8	K8	KB8	KKt8	KR8
QR7	QKt7	QB7	Q7	K7	KB7	KKt7	KR7
QR6	QKt6	QB6	Q6	K6	KB6	KKt6	KR6
QR5	QKt5	QB5	Q5	K5	KB5	KKt5	KR5
QR4	QKt4	QB4	Q4	K4	KB4	KKt4	KR4
QR3	QKt3	QB3	Q3	K3	KB3	KKt3	KR3
QR2	QKt2	QB2	Q2	K2	KB2	KKt2	KR2
QR1	QKt1	QB1	Q1	K1	KB1	KKt1	KR1

Labels for White

9

QR1	QKt1	QB1	Q1	K1	KB1	KKt1	KR1
QR2	QKt2	QB2	Q2	K2	KB2	KKt2	KR2
QR3	QKt3	QB3	Q3	K3	KB3	KKt3	KR3
QR4	QKt4	QB4	Q4	K4	KB4	KKt4	KR4
QR5	QKt5	QB5	Q5	K5	KB5	KKt5	KR5
QR6	QKt6	QB6	Q6	K6	KB6	KKt6	KR6
QR7	QKt7	QB7	Q7	K7	KB7	KKt7	KR7
QR8	QKt8	QB8	Q8	K8	KB8	KKt8	KR8

Labels for Black

When reference is made in the book to the number of a square, it is the combination of the initial letters of the piece and the rank number which determine what this is, e.g. KB3, meaning the third rank square of the King's Bishop's file, or QR4, meaning the fourth rank square of the Queen's Rook's file. The notation will always relate to either White's moves or Black's moves, so that when we say White's Rook on Q1, we refer to the square Q1 as seen from White's viewpoint, and similarly if we refer to Black's Rook on Q1, we mean the square Q1 as seen from Black's side of the board.

Practice

Without reference to relevant diagrams in the book, write out the square labels for both White and Black. Place a few pieces at random on the chessboard, and calculate the square numbers they rest upon; white labels for white pieces, and black labels for black pieces.

TEST 1

(Solutions at end of book)

Setting up the pieces on their starting squares; ranks, files and diagonals; King's side, Queen's side; *j'adoube*; labelling the squares.

Q.1. How many straight lines of squares are there on the chessboard?*

Q.2. How many straight lines of *eight squares* are there on a chess-board?*

Q.3. If two players find, at the start of a game, that the pieces have been set up with the board the wrong way round (black square instead of white in the bottom right-hand corner) is there a way of turning the board round or sideways in order to put things right, avoiding the need to move the pieces into fresh lines?*

Q.4. If you were to set up the chessboard with all the pieces except Pawns on their starting squares, which pieces would be facing their opposite numbers along the files at the other end of the board, and which not?

Q.5. If you are White, is the Queen's side of the board on your left-hand side, or right-hand side?

Q.6. What penalty may be exacted if it is your opponent's turn to move and you adjust a piece on its square, without giving prior warning of your intention?

Q.7. Indicate on your chessboard:

    (i) White's second rank;

    (ii) White's fifth rank;

    (iii) Black's seventh rank;

    (iv) the Queen's file;

    (v) the King's file.

* In answering this question, you may refer to the diagrams on pages 14 to 16.

Q.8. Give the square numbers, first from White's point of view and then for Black's, of all the squares marked ϕ in Diagram 10. To assist, we have divided the diagram into Queen's side and King's side and given the square numbers of the left hand first rank square for both Black and White sides of the board (QR1 for White and KR1 for Black).

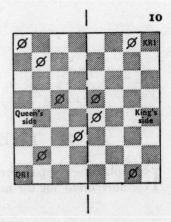

Do not proceed to the next part of the book until you have correctly understood the principles involved in Questions 3, 4, 5, 6 and 7.

White Queen starts on a white square, black Queen starts on a black square—'Queen on her square, same coloured pair'!

CHAPTER 3

HOW THE CHESSMEN MOVE

IN explaining the patterns of movement of the pieces, we are going to consider them, for the moment, away from their starting positions.

Move of the King

The King may, in one move, go one square in any direction.

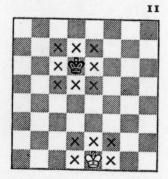

II

The King shown on the nearside of the board may move to any one of five squares. Anywhere away from the side of the board it may move to any one of eight squares, as shown. The King has the most limited choice of moves when situated on a corner square.

Practice

Discover from which positions on the board the King may move to only three squares; then squares from which it may move to only five squares, then to eight squares.

Move of the Rook

The Rook may, in one move, go in a straight line, anywhere along the rank or file on which it stands.

22

12

The Rook is able to move to any one of fourteen squares wherever it stands on an empty chessboard. All ranks and files are shown in the diagrams on page 16.

Practice

Confirm by experiment that the Rook may move to fourteen squares, never more, never less, wherever it is placed on an empty chessboard.

Attacking and Capturing

If any piece, except a Pawn (Pawn attacking and capturing will be dealt with later), is able to occupy a square on the next move, such a square is said to be attacked by the piece. In Diagram 13 we see the attacking power of King and Rook. Squares attacked by the King are marked ϕ, whilst those attacked by the Rook are marked $\times$.

13

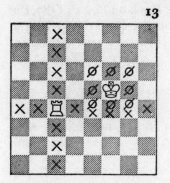

Attacking power of King and Rook. *Both* pieces attack White's K4, KB4 and KKt4.

One square at a time for the King—Ranks and files for the Rook!

Suppose we have a position in which the two white pieces in Diagram 13 are joined by two black Rooks. *See* Diagram 14. It is White's turn to move.

14

White to play

The white Rook at QB4 attacks squares QB8, QB7, QB6, QB5 and QB3 along the file, and QR4, QKt4, Q4, K4 and KB4 along the rank. This Rook also attacks the black Rook at Black's QB7, and the second Rook at KKt5. White's QB1 (marked NA) is *not attacked* by the white Rook because of the blocking action of the black Rook at QB7. Similarly White's KR4 is beyond the scope of the white Rook, as a result of the position of the black Rook at KKt5. Find out for yourself other squares blocked from attack in this position.

Since the white King is attacking white square KKt4, the black Rook now standing on this square (which is Black's KKt5) may be captured and removed from the board. In this case, the white King then occupies KKt4, in place of the Rook. Alternatively, White may capture this Rook with the white Rook at QB4. Yet a third alternative capture is possible in this position, for the white Rook may also capture the other black Rook at Black's QB7. Naturally, you are not allowed to capture one of your own pieces! There is no compulsion for a player to capture a piece he is attacking.

Should White finally decide to capture the Rook on Black's QB7, the latter piece is removed from the board, the capturing Rook occupying the square so vacated. The resulting position would be as shown in Diagram 15.

15

The diagram shows the position after the white Rook has captured the Rook at Black's QB7.

You will find there are three ways of getting out of attack:

(i) blocking the attack with another piece;

(ii) capturing the attacker;

(iii) moving the attacked piece out of the attack.

Check and Checkmate

1. Check

When a player attacks a King, the King is said to be in check. It is usual and courteous, but not compulsory, for the attacker to say 'Check' when attacking the King.

When a player is in check, he must, unless it is impossible, reply by getting out of check *on the next move*. A player may not make a move which puts himself in check, and if he does so inadvertently his opponent should point out the illegality of the move.

In the following position (Diagram 16) the white King is in check by the Rook on Black's square Q6:

16

White's King is in check by the black Rook.

White has three ways of getting out of check:

Three ways of getting out of attack!

(i) *Move the King.* King moves to QB6, QB7, QB8 or K6. Since you are not allowed to put yourself in check, the white King is not permitted to move to either square K7 or K8, since these squares are attacked by the black King. You will notice that, following the rule of check, two Kings may never occupy adjoining squares.

(ii) *Capture the attacker.* Capture the attacker with the white Rook at QKt3.

(iii) *Block the attack.* Play the white Rook at QKt6 to Q6.

If the position in Diagram 16 were reached in an actual game, White would be forced to adopt one of the three courses just outlined. It would be illegal for White to make a move which left his King in check.

2. Checkmate

In the event that a King is attacked and unable to get out of the attack, it is checkmate, and the game is over.

17

White to play

In the position shown (Diagram 17), White may give checkmate in one move.

White plays the Rook to KR1 checkmate. The black King may not, of course, escape to Black's KKt3, KKt2 or KKt1, for these squares are attacked by the white King. Any move by the black King would, therefore, be into check, and this is illegal.

Because of the rule of check, the two opposing Kings may never occupy adjoining squares!

Checkmate! No escape for the black King.

The King may not be removed from the board during the course of a game.

Practice
Invent positions of attack, involving check and checkmate, using Kings and Rooks. You will find that checkmate with a King and Rook against a lone King usually forms a pattern in which the losing King, always on the side of the board, directly faces the opposing King. Find the checkmate pattern, still using the same pieces as in Diagram 18, in which the two Kings do *not* directly face each other.

TEST 2
(*Solutions at end of book*)
Moves of the King and Rook; attacking and capturing; check and checkmate.

19

Q.1. Which squares are attacked by the white pieces in the position shown in Diagram 19?

If you can get out of check on the next move, you **must!!**

20

Q.2. What possible capturing moves are open to Black in the position shown in Diagram 20?

21

Q.3. What choice of move has White in the position shown in Diagram 21?

White to play

Q.4. How would you know that it was White to play in the position shown in Diagram 21, even if the fact had not been stated?

Q.5. If you have correctly answered Q.3, it should not be difficult to find a strong black move to follow. See if you can find the move.

Q.6. Add a white King and white Rook to accompany the black King already shown in Diagram 22, so as to create a position of checkmate. Try the Rook in several positions and see how many separate patterns of checkmate you can find.

22

Do not proceed to the next part of the book until you have correctly understood the principles involved in all the questions of this test.

In check and unable to escape? Checkmate!

Move of the Bishop

The Bishop may, in one move, go in a straight line, anywhere along the diagonal on which it stands. All the diagonals are shown in Diagrams 6 and 7 on page 16.

23

Attacking pattern of the Bishop.

A Bishop which starts on a white square (known as the 'white square' Bishop) moves along white diagonals only. A Bishop which starts on a black square ('black square' Bishop) moves only along black diagonals.

If an enemy piece stands on a square attacked by a Bishop, the Bishop may capture it, occupying the square on which the captured piece stood. In the following position the black square Bishop may move to any of the squares arrowed, or capture the attacked Rook which stands on Black's KB7.

24

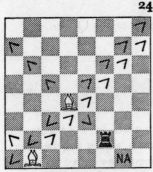

White to play

White's black square Bishop attacks the Rook. White's KKt1, marked NA, is not attacked by this Bishop, because of the blocking action of the Rook.

If White captures the Rook, the Bishop replaces the captured piece which is removed from the board.

29

You will remember that a Rook may move to any one of fourteen squares, wherever it is placed on an empty chessboard. The power of the Bishop, however, varies according to its position on the chessboard. Had the Rook not been on the board in the position shown in Diagram 24, the black square Bishop would have been able to attack thirteen squares. The other Bishop attacks only seven squares. As in the case of the Rook, the Bishop may not, in one move, turn a corner.

Practice

Place the Bishops in various positions on the chessboard, and compare squares from which they enjoy maximum square attacking power with squares where they have little power.

Experiment with two Bishops of the same side, placing them side by side, forming a solid barrier of attack. Check the effectiveness of this barrier by seeing if it is possible for the opposing King to cross it. (Remember a King may not move into check.)

Move of the Queen

The Queen may, in one move, go in a straight line anywhere along the rank, file or diagonal on which it stands. All the ranks, files and diagonals are illustrated in Diagrams 4 to 7 on page 16.

25

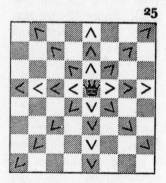

Attacking pattern of the Queen.

If an enemy piece stands on a square attacked by a Queen, the Queen may capture it, occupying the square on which the captured piece stood. In the following position the Queen may move to any of the squares arrowed, or capture the attacked Bishop which stands on White's KB5.

Diagonals for Bishops!

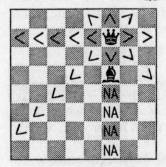

Queen attacks Bishop. Squares marked NA are not attacked because of the blocking action of the Bishop on the King's Bishop's file.

If Black captures the Bishop, the Queen replaces the captured piece which is removed from the board.

Like the Bishop, the power of the Queen varies according to its position on the chessboard. In Diagram 25 the Queen attacks *twenty-seven* squares, while the Queen in Diagram 26 attacks only *nineteen* squares. Had the Bishop not been on the board, the Queen in Diagram 26 would have been able to attack *twenty-three* squares.

Practice

Place the Queen in various positions of the chessboard, and compare squares from which it may enjoy maximum square attacking power, with squares where it has little square attacking power.

Place a Queen on a square from which it may attack the maximum number of twenty-seven squares. Then remove the Queen from the board and replace it with a Rook and a Bishop of the same side. Find out whether these two pieces in combined action anywhere on the chessboard are able to match the square attacking power of the Queen.

Move of the Knight

The Knight is the only piece which appears to turn a corner when it moves. Moreover, it is the only piece which appears to jump over other pieces! The move of the Knight may be likened to the shape of

Ranks, files and diagonals for Queens!

the letter L. The move shape as illustrated below may be upside-down, sideways or back to front. The Knight moves from one end of the L shape to the other. Here are the shapes in all their forms:

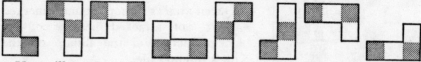

You will see that when a Knight moves from a white square it lands on a black square; if it stands on a black square it moves to a white square.

Another way of thinking of the direction of the Knight move is:

> one square along the rank or file on which it stands, then two squares at right angles,

or

> two squares along the rank or file, then one square at right angles.

In Diagram 27 you will see that in or towards the centre of the board the Knight attacks eight squares. In the corner, the Knight's choice of move is limited to two squares, whilst elsewhere on the edge of the board it attacks either three or four squares.

27

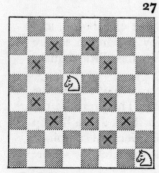

Attacking power of the Knight.

In Diagram 28 we see the peculiar ability of the Knight to jump over other pieces.

28

The Knight may move to either QKt3 or QB2, despite the fact that it may look, at first sight, to be shut in.

In one move, a Knight is able both to jump and turn a corner!

32

In Diagram 29 an enemy Bishop stands on one of the squares attacked by the Knight. Should the Knight capture the Bishop, the Bishop would be removed from the board, the Knight occupying the square so vacated.

29

Knight attacks Bishop.

Unlike the Rook, Bishop and Queen, which attack along straight lines, *the attack of the Knight may not be blocked.*

Practice

Place the Knights in various positions on the chessboard, and compare squares from which they enjoy maximum power with squares from which they have little power.

Invent positions such as that in Diagram 28, in which a Knight has to cross other pieces in order to move.

Determine by experiment that it is impossible to block the attack of a Knight.

Place a white Knight on square QB5 and find out the fewest number of moves it takes for the Knight to reach QB6, QKt5, QB4 or Q5 (adjoining squares on rank and file). From White's QB5 find the fewest number of moves a Knight takes to reach QKt6, Q6, QKt4 and Q4 (adjoining squares on the diagonal). From QB5 find out the fewest number of moves a Knight takes to reach K7, QR7, QR3 or K3 (next square but one, along the diagonal).

Move of the Pawn

Any Pawn which has not left its starting square may, on its *first* move only, go forward along the file *either one or two squares.* Thereafter, the Pawn may continue to advance along the file *one* square at a time

33

only. The Pawn is the only piece which may not move backwards; it may not jump over pieces.

30

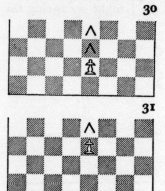

On its first move, a choice of one or two squares forward.

31

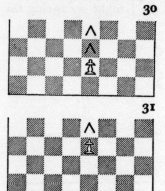

Here, the Pawn may advance only one square, for it has already been moved.

A Pawn which, on its way to the queening square, is not blocked by an opposing Pawn and does not have to cross a square attacked by an enemy Pawn on an adjoining file, is known as a 'passed' Pawn.

Queening a Pawn

When a Pawn reaches the eighth rank it *must* be changed to any other piece of the same colour (except a King). Since the Queen has the most powerful attacking strength of all the pieces, the change is usually to a Queen, and it is for this reason that the promotion of a Pawn is known as 'queening'.

32   **33**

The Pawn moves to the eighth rank and becomes a Queen.

The Pawn is removed and is replaced by a Queen, all in *one* move.

A Pawn may be promoted to a Queen regardless of whether a Queen of the same colour already exists on the board. The same principle applies to the other pieces. It is, therefore, possible to have extra Queens, Rooks, Bishops and Knights on the board at the same time, as the result of a number of such Pawn promotions.

One or two squares forward on a Pawn's first move!

34

Attacking and Capturing by Pawns

All pieces, except Pawns, capture in the same way as their ordinary moves. Although Pawns normally move forward along the files, they do not attack or capture in this way. To capture, a Pawn moves diagonally forward one square, to either adjacent file.

34

The Pawn attacks both the Rook and the Knight.

The Pawn in Diagram 34 has the choice of three moves:

(i) to square QKt4 capturing the Rook;
(ii) to square Q4 capturing the Knight;
(iii) to square QB4 along the file, making no capture.

In a wider position which incorporates the situation illustrated in Diagram 34 Black is not, of course, forced to make any move at all with the Pawn, unless such a move is the only one at his disposal. Should the white Rook be captured by the Pawn, the latter would, thereafter, be known as the QKt Pawn and not QB Pawn as hitherto. Similarly, if the Knight were captured by the Pawn, it would be known as the Queen's Pawn. We go into more detail concerning the identification of Pawns later in the book.

In Diagram 35 the position is similar to that in Diagram 34, except that the black Pawn's progress along the Bishop's file is blocked by the Pawn on White's QB5.

35

The white Pawn now blocks the advance of the black Pawn along the file on which it stands. The only move the black Pawn may now make is to capture either the Rook or the Knight.

36

The position if Black captures the Rook.

Pawn Capture *en passant**

This special capturing move is a surviving link with earlier times when Pawns were allowed to move only one square forward on the first move. The change to the present rule, which permits the choice of one or two squares of advance for the Pawn on its first move, was made in order to speed up the game.

Look at the position in Diagram 37, in which the black Pawn 'passes over' Black's Q3, which is attacked by White's Pawn:

37

38

The black Pawn moves forward two squares on its first move. Provided he does so on his *next move*, White may now capture *en passant*.

Position after White has captured *en passant*. *The white Pawn has captured the black Pawn as though the latter had moved forward only one square.*

After Black's move in the position shown in Diagram 37 White is not, of course, compelled to capture the black Pawn. Note that the capturing Pawn must be on the fifth rank in all *en passant* captures.

A player may capture *en passant* more than once in a game; in fact he may so capture whenever his opponent makes a two-square Pawn move to the side of one of his own Pawns. Remember that capture *en passant* must take place on the move *immediately following* the two-square move of the Pawn to be captured.

* *en passant* is French for 'in passing'.

The only piece which may never move backwards? The Pawn!

Practice

Set up the board with only the Pawns. Practise 'limited' games either on your own, or with a friend, in which the Pawns are advanced, and captures made. See which side 'queens' the most Pawns. Include, where possible, single and double square initial moves, as well as *en passant* captures and queening.

Castling

Once during the course of a game, a player may make a special move which is intended to transfer the King to a place of comparative safety and at the same time develop a Rook towards the files which run through the centre of the board. This movement is known as 'castling' and allows the King to move two squares towards either Rook of the same colour, whilst the Rook concerned goes round to the other side of the King. This double movement counts as *one move*. The following diagrams show how castling works for Black and White:

39

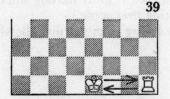

40

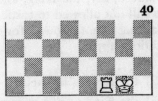

The white King and King's Rook on their starting squares are ready to castle.

Position after castling on the King's side (recorded O—O; *see also* p. 46).

Castling on the Queen's side is carried out in a similar way:

41

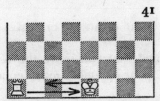

42

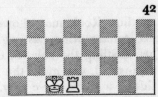

The King moves two squares towards the Queen's Rook and the Rook comes round to the other side of the King.

White has castled Queen's side (recorded O—O—O; *see also* p. 46).

Diagrams 43 and 44 show King's side and Queen's side castling for Black:

43

44

Black has castled King's side (O—O).

Black has castled Queen's side (O—O—O).

Castling is allowed only once in a game by both Black and White and there are several kinds of situation in which you are not allowed to castle, either for the time being or for the rest of the game.

If either your King or the Rook concerned has been moved from its starting square, **castling may not take place at all.** (If a player has moved, say, the King, and later returned it to its starting square, he is still not allowed to castle at all during that game.)

Castling is not allowed **for the time being** if any of the following conditions apply:

  (i) the King is in check;

  (ii) the King would be moving into check;

(iii) the King would have to cross an attacked square;

(iv) a piece is standing on a square between the King and the castling Rook.

The castling Rook may, however, move out of attack or across an attacked square, when castling.

When castling the rules of chess demand that you move the King first. If, instead, you move the Rook first, your opponent may demand that this be a Rook move only.

The following diagrams illustrate some conditions in which castling is prevented. The reader should assume that the Kings and Rooks concerned in the following illustrations have not been previously moved from their starting squares:

White is prevented from castling for the rest of the game.

White is prevented from castling for the time being.

45

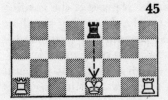

Since the King is in check and must move to get out of check, White will not be able to castle at all during the game.

46

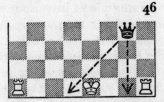

White is prevented from castling for the time being because of the attack of the Queen. To attempt to castle King's side would mean the King moving into check, whilst to castle Queen's side would involve the King in crossing an attacked square. Either of these moves would be illegal.

In Diagram 47 Black may castle Queen's side, for in castling the Rook concerned is allowed to cross an attacked square. Since castling King's side would mean the King crossing an attacked square, King's side castling is not possible. Should the Bishop move away from attack against Black's KB1, to, say, White's K5, castling would then be permitted King's side or Queen's side.

47

48

Castling permitted Queen's side, but temporarily prevented on the King's side.

Black may not castle King's side since one of the squares separating the King and King's Rook is occupied by a piece. Castling is, however, possible Queen's side.

When castling, make sure you move the King first!

Practice

Set up positions in which castling is possible, then place opposing pieces in various positions which prevent the castling move, either temporarily or permanently. In setting up these positions, remember that castling is permanently prevented if the King or Rook concerned has previously been moved.

Invent positions where an attack, which temporarily prevents castling, may be blocked in such a way that castling becomes possible.

TEST 3

(Solutions at end of book)

Moves of Bishop, Queen, Knight and Pawn, including capture, *en passant* and queening; castling.

Q.1. Given an otherwise empty chessboard and an unlimited number of moves, the Rook could attack or occupy every square of the chessboard. What proportion of the squares of the chessboard may be attacked or occupied by a single Bishop?

Q.2. Given the unlimited opportunities of moves described in Q.1, state what proportion of the squares of the chessboard may be attacked or occupied by:

 (i) a Queen;

(ii) a Knight.

Q.3. Given an otherwise empty chessboard and the most favourable square of occupation, which piece is able, in one move, to attack the greatest number of squares?

Q.4. What is the maximum number of squares which may be attacked, in one move, by a single Pawn?

Castle early—it tucks your King away to safety!

3. A chess clock, as used in competitions where the time factor is important. It really consists of two connected clocks, each operating independently with a stop-watch action. This ensures that each player's thinking time is recorded. A specified minimum number of moves, as a rule not more than 24, must be played in the first hour and a further appropriate number of moves for each ensuing half-hour or quarter-hour; or, say, 48 moves to two hours. Failing to keep pace with the clock at previously agreed time checks loses the game. The illustration shows that the knob on the right-hand clock face has been depressed, which indicates that the right-hand clock has been stopped and that the left-hand one is operating. Adjacent to the figure eight on each clock face is a 'ticker' which is activated when the clock is working. The ticker on the left-hand clock face would be the one in movement. Between the 11 and 12 on each clock face is a 'flag'. On the right-hand clock face, the minute hand has begun to raise the flag; on the hour the flag will fall. (*See also* p. 119.)

Q.5. Which piece (not counting Pawns) does not increase its square attacking power the nearer it is to the four centre squares of the chessboard?

Q.6. In each of the following four positions (Diagrams 49 to 52) you are required to attack the white King with the piece indicated, in such a way that checkmate is given. It is Black to play in each case:

49

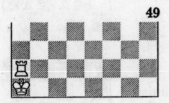

From which square could a black Queen give checkmate?

50

Find the two squares from which a black Knight may give checkmate.

51

Find the square from which Black's black square Bishop may give checkmate.

52

In this position all the relevant pieces are shown. How may Black give checkmate next move?

53

Q.7. White has just played the Pawn from QKt3 to QKt4. Is Black able to capture *en passant*?

41

54

Q.8. In this position only one Pawn may move. Identify the Pawn and describe the only move which it would be possible for it to make.

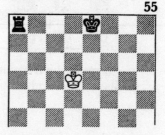

55

Q.9. In castling, Black would be putting White in check. Is such a castling move legal?

Q.10. Which piece should be moved first, in the act of castling?

Do not proceed to the next part of the book until you have correctly understood the principles involved in all the questions of this test.

Although a miniature chess set is useful in its place, it is a poor substitute for a full sized set of pieces and board, both for games and for playing through the instructive positions and test questions in this book!

CHAPTER 4

VALUES OF THE PIECES

IF you have practised with all the pieces in order to examine the scope of their attacking power, you will soon have found that in matters of attack, capture and checkmate, some pieces are very much more useful than others. Since, in the course of most games, captures and exchanges occur, it is important to understand the relative values of the pieces.

It is impossible to give any piece a *fixed* value, since its importance will vary as the game progresses. For example, a piece entirely blocked-in and valueless at one stage of the game, may later emerge to be of supreme importance. A piece which has taken, say, three necessary moves to reach a square from which it has good attacking possibilities, is worth much more than a similar piece which is undeveloped and ineffective. Consider, again, the varying power of the Pawn, which grows in stature the nearer it gets to the queening square! Nevertheless, in the general run of play during a game, some pieces are actually or potentially of greater value than others, and the following table of approximate values may be a useful guide:

The Pawn	. worth 1 unit	
The Queen	. worth 9 units	major pieces
The Rook	. worth 5 units	
The Bishop	. worth 3 units	minor pieces
The Knight	. worth 3 units	

Remember that this assessment is only a rough guide; the real values of the pieces at any given time depend on where they are placed on the chessboard. If a player has a single Pawn move at his disposal which may give checkmate, then the value of the Pawn is inestimable, despite its low reckoning in the above scale. Pieces are able to exercise their power to the full, only when they occupy strong and active positions.

It is up to you to extract the greatest possible usefulness from your chess army, by positioning your forces securely, where they have the maximum hitting power.

Practice

Set up positions in which piece exchanges take place. Play the captures over and determine whether they have been worthwhile.

Experiment by playing 'games' in which only some of the pieces are set up. Play King, Queen and three Pawns against King, two Rooks and three Pawns. King, Knight and three Pawns against King, Bishop and three Pawns is another useful exercise.

Invent your own combinations of pieces for the two sides and play one against the other. Try to ensure that if you have to give up a piece, that your sacrifice is worthwhile, even if you have to wait sometime for the return. Never give anything away for nothing!

When you make an exchange of pieces, ensure you get good value!

CHAPTER 5

KEEPING A RECORD OF MOVES

Y ou have already learned to identify the squares of the chess-board (*see* page 18). To record the move of a piece to an empty square, simply state the initial letter(s) of the piece being moved, followed by a dash and the square of arrival, i.e. 'White plays Q—Q2' indicates the move of the white Queen to vacant square Q2. Remember that when the square of a white piece is referred to, a white square number is used and a black square number for a black piece. In the case of a capture, the initial letter of the piece making the capture is given, followed by the capturing sign '×' and the initial letter of the piece being captured. 'Black plays R × B' indicates the capture of a white Bishop by a black Rook.

Should it be possible for either of Black's Rooks to make the capture of the Bishop in the previous example, to avoid confusion, the move may be recorded with the King's side or Queen's side identification letter, i.e. '*Q*R(or *K*R) × B', or should the Rook be able to capture either of White's Bishops, then 'QR × *K*B or *Q*B'. Although this example is of a capture, the same principle applies to any move which might be ambiguous. In cases where there might be doubt as to whether the piece concerned is the Queen's side or King's side piece, the square number of the piece being moved may be given, i.e. 'R(R1) × B'.

A Pawn, in moving to an adjoining file when capturing, takes on the identity of the new file. For example, a King's Pawn in capturing the enemy Queen's Pawn then becomes known as a Queen's Pawn, upon entering the Queen's file. In the event that there are two Pawns of the same colour on a file, where desirable, the square number of the Pawn concerned may be added to the recording, i.e. 'P(Q4) × P'.

To denote the promotion of a Pawn to Queen, the initial letter 'Q' follows the recording of the Pawn move, e.g. 'P—K8 = Q' or 'P × R

45

= Q'. The initial letters '*e.p.*' follow the particulars of an *en passant* capture, e.g. 'P×P *e.p.*'.

The following is a list of the symbols commonly used in describing the moves of a game:

—	moves to
×	captures
O—O	castles King's side
O—O—O	castles Queen's side
e.p.	*en passant*
ch.	check
mate	checkmate
!	good move, e.g. P—K6!
?	poor move, e.g. R—Q4?

Reference to such terms as 'White wins' or 'White has winning chances', which you may find in chess books and periodicals, means that although no immediate checkmate is available, White should be able to force or has some chances of forcing, checkmate, in due course.

To assist beginners in understanding chess notation, we have, for the sake of clarity, occasionally given references in more detail than would normally be necessary.

There follows a game played in the 1905 British Championship. Play the moves over on a chessboard, and check your progress in interpreting the notation, by referring to Diagrams 56 to 59, which show the positions reached after Black's 5th move, 8th move, 15th move, as well as the final position. In serious matches and tournaments, specially printed score sheets are used for the recording of games. Beginners who wish to record their friendly games for subsequent study may find books of score sheets useful (*see* Plate 4).

Game 1

White	**Black**
J. H. Blackburne	Sherrard
1 P—K4	

It is not necessary to state which Pawn, for only one Pawn may go to White's K4.

1 ...	P—K4

Record your more serious games; analyse and profit from your weaknesses!

The row of dots indicates that this is a black move. The dots are used only when there might be confusion as to whether a move referred to is a white move or a black move.

White	Black
2 P—KB4	

Since both of White's Bishop's Pawns may go to B4, it is necessary to identify which Pawn is referred to. Although the moves of this game are given in column form, with white moves on the left and black moves on the right, they are sometimes shown along the line. The moves already played in this game would, recorded along the line, read: '1 P—K4, P—K4; 2 P—KB4'.

2 ...	P—Q4
3 Kt—KB3	

Once again we need to identify with the 'K', that the B3 square referred to is the one on the King's side.

3 ...	QP×P

Black captures a Pawn. 'P×P' would be ambiguous, since Black may capture a Pawn with either the King's Pawn or Queen's Pawn.

4 Kt×P	

Only one Knight (KB3) may capture only one pawn (Black's K4), so we have no need to say which Knight is concerned.

4 ...	B—Q3
5 P—Q4	P×P *e.p.*

Black captures White's Queen's Pawn with the Pawn on Black's K5. *See* Diagram 56.

56

Position after 5 ... P×P *e.p.*

This is the position you should have reached after five moves on both sides.

6 B×P

No need to state which Pawn is captured here, for only one Bishop (KB1) may capture only one Pawn (Black's Q6).

White	Black
6 ...	Kt—KB3

It is necessary to state *KB*3 for either of Black's Knights may go to a B3 square.

| 7 O—O | O—O |

Both sides have castled King's side.

8 Kt—QB3

Either white Knight may go to a B3 square.

| 8 ... | QKt—Q2 |

Either Knight may go to this square. *See* Diagram 57.

57

Position after 8 ...QKt—Q2

Position after eight moves on both sides.

| 9 Kt×Kt | B×Kt |
| 10 P—B5 | |

Only the KB Pawn may go to the fifth rank.

| 10 ... | B—B3 |
| 11 B—KKt5 | |

White square labels for white pieces; black square labels for black pieces!

48

Notice that the other white Bishop may also go to Kt5.

White	Black
11 ...	P—KR3
12 B—R4	R—K1
13 R—K1	B—K4

See Diagram 58.

58

Position after thirteen moves on both sides.

Position after 13 ... B—K4

	White	Black
14	B—K2	B—Q5 ch.
15	K—R1	Kt—K5
16	Kt×Kt	Q×B
17	Q×B	R×Kt
18	Q—Q2	Q—B7
19	P—B6	R×B
20	Q×R	B×P mate

See Diagram 59.

59

The final position shows an example of checkmate given by a minor piece supported by the Queen.

Final position after
20 ... B×P mate

4

Practice

Record and replay some of your friendly games with a sympathetic and patient opponent (games take a little longer when the moves are being recorded).

If you wish to read other chess books, learn to identify as soon as possible, the ranks, files and squares, without having to refer to the labelled diagrams in this book. Few competitive players record their games without the occasional error in notation. A thorough study and plenty of practice in notation will greatly benefit those who wish to take the game seriously, for much time may be lost in trying to retrieve the course of incorrectly scored games.

Record your games so that you may replay them and learn from your mistakes!

CHAPTER 6

PATTERNS OF CHECKMATE

Now that all the moves of the pieces have been explained, we will look at them in checkmate action.

King and Rook Against King

We have already seen the pattern of Rook checkmating with King support (Diagram 18). Let us look at the method White adopted to drive the black King to the edge of the board:

60

White's task is to drive the lone King to the edge of the board. The position of the two Kings facing each other across the file is instructive, for the defending King is now forced by White's attacking pattern, towards the side of the board.

Black to play

Here is one way in which the black King may be checkmated:

White	Black
1 ...	K—B4
2 K—Q4	K—B3
3 R—K5	

This move restricts the black King to an area of only nine squares of the chessboard.

White	Black
3 ...	K—B2
4 K—K4	K—B3
5 K—B4	K—Kt3
6 R—B5	

The black King has now been restricted to six squares.

White	Black
6 ...	K—R3
7 R—Kt5	

The black King now has only three squares left.

7 ...	K—R2
8 K—B5	K—R3
9 K—B6	K—R2
10 R—Kt1	

If Black now plays 10 ... K—R3, we have the position similar to the pattern in Diagram 60, and now White may follow with 11 R—R1 checkmate. If, instead of 10 R—Kt1 White had played 10 K—B7, Black would reply 10 ... K—R3 and, for the time being, at any rate, escapes the mating net. It is to prepare the way for the final checkmating move on the Rook's file *by making the black King move into the pattern described in Diagram 60*, that White has played a 'waiting' move down the Knight's file. White's tenth move was to Kt1, but Kt2, Kt3 or Kt4 would have served the purpose just as well.

10 ...	K—R1
11 K—B7	

61

Black to play

Black's only move is to allow the two Kings to face each other across the file, as illustrated in Diagram 60.

11 ...	K—R2
12 R—R1 mate	

We have reached the position which illustrated checkmate on page 27, Diagram 18.

King and Queen Against King
Look at the following position (Diagram 62):

62

Black to play

The position is the same as that in Diagram 60, except that we have a white Queen on K1 instead of a Rook.

The following shows one way in which White may force checkmate.

White	Black
1 ...	K—B4
2 K—Q4	K—B3
3 Q—K5 ch	

Restricting the black King to the same small corner of the board as in the Rook variation after White's 3rd move.

3 ...	K—B2
4 K—K4	K—Kt1
5 Q—K7	

This move restricts the black King to two squares of his first rank.

5 ...	K—R1
6 K—B5	K—Kt1
7 K—Kt6	K—R1
8 Q—Q8, K8, B8, Kt7 or R7 mate!	

These two examples emphasise the greater power the Queen has compared with that of the Rook.

With King supported by Queen or Rook against King, confine the defending King to an ever-decreasing area of the board.

53

There follow other patterns of checkmate, showing all the pieces in action. In some of the patterns you will see that the attacked King's escape is blocked by defending pieces. Learn to recognise the patterns, so that you will be able to use the ideas they incorporate in the games you play.

63

Rook mates on the eighth rank, helped by the defending Pawns!

64

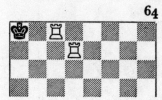

Mate using Rooks on adjoining ranks. One Rook attacks, the other cuts off the escape.

65

Mate using self-supporting Rooks. The black Rook occupies a square, which if vacant, would have allowed the King's escape.

66

Mate with self-supporting Rooks on the Knight's file. The black Rook again helps to block the King's escape.

67

Rook mates supported by Pawn on QB6.

68

This mate is sometimes known as a 'corridor' mate. Easy to see why it has this name!

Checkmate patterns do not just happen in play—you have to create them!

69

Queen mates with Rook support.

70

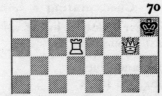

Queen mates with Rook support.

71

Queen mates with Pawn support.

72

Rook mates with Knight support.

73

Rook mates with Bishop support.

74

Rook mates with Bishop support.

75

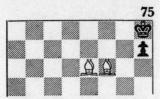

Mate with two Bishops.

76

This mate by a Knight is known as 'smothered' mate.

Practice

Construct patterns of checkmate similar to those illustrated. Invent checkmate situations using the minimum number of pieces.

Create these patterns in the games you play in order to force checkmate as soon as possible.

55

Checkmating a Lone King—Minimum Forces

We give below a list of minimum forces necessary for checkmate against a lone King:

King and Queen
King and Rook

King and two Bishops
King, Knight and Bishop
King and three Knights

{ Examples of these checkmates are so rare that you are advised not to examine their possibilities until you are well beyond the beginner stage.

It follows from a consideration of the above table that against a lone King, you cannot checkmate with only a King and two Knights, King and Knight, King and Bishop—or an unaided King.

Remember that the forces outlined in the minimum force table do not take into account the help sometimes afforded by defending pieces which may cut off the escape of the attacked King. Checkmate may often be forced with fewer pieces than those referred to in the above table, if the attack is assisted by the blocking action of enemy pieces (e.g. *see* Diagrams 63, 65, etc.). Naturally, if the attacking force is greater than the minimum requirement, checkmate should be easier to effect.

How can you have three Knights of one colour? By Pawn promotion!

CHAPTER 7

DRAWN GAMES

Not all games of chess may be won or lost. Quite often so many pieces on both sides become captured that neither side has sufficient material left with which to force checkmate. In this case the result is a draw. In order to save time, a draw is sometimes mutually agreed between opponents who consider this to be a fair and inevitable result, despite the fact that both sides may possess more than the minimum forces necessary for checkmate.

Another example of a drawn game is when a player, whose turn it is to move, finds he cannot, although he is not in check. This kind of situation is known as 'stalemate'. The following position shows how stalemate may be forced in order to gain a draw in a position which might otherwise be lost:

77

White to play

Black is winning easily in material, but White has a resource.

1 R—KR8 ch., K × R stalemate. White is unable to move, and yet is not in check. Game drawn.

Yet a further way of arriving at a draw occurs when the same position is reached three times in a game, with the same player to move each time. The most common kind of situation under this rule is when a player is able to check his opponent non-stop. This continuous checking is called perpetual check. *See* Diagram 78.

78

Black to play

Although White has a clear winning advantage in material, Black manages to avoid losing!

1 ...	Q—QR5 ch
2 K—Kt1	Q—Q8 ch
3 K—R2	Q—R5 ch

and so on non-stop! The game is drawn by perpetual check.

Other and more complicated examples of the rule concerning the repetition of moves may occur very occasionally, when it is necessary to refer to the official laws of the game, but it is recommended that further consideration of the rule be postponed until you have advanced beyond the 'beginner' stage.

There is one more way of reaching a drawn position. This occurs when fifty moves have been made on both sides, and no capture made, nor Pawn moved. It may happen, for example, that a player has a mating force advantage against an opponent who has, say, no piece, other than his King. Should the player with the advantage be unable to checkmate his opponent, the latter may count the moves; if, after fifty moves, checkmate has still not been forced, a draw may be claimed.

The following is a summary of ways in which games may be drawn:

   (i) by mutual consent;
  (ii) insufficient force for checkmate;
 (iii) stalemate;
  (iv) position repeated three times (including perpetual check);
   (v) fifty move rule.

Practice

Invent positions in which the player who has the move, though not in check, is unable to move (stalemate). Offer such positions to a friend to see if he is able to find legal moves for the sides you consider to be in stalemate.

Invent positions in which stalemate may be forced.

Invent positions in which it is possible to check non-stop (perpetual check).

During across-the-board play, avoid carelessly offering your opponents stalemate opportunities, in positions from which you should have won.

Set up the position, with Black to play, in which the black King is on Q5, a black Queen on QKt6 and the white King on QR1. Now force checkmate, not stalemate! Note that if on Black's first move you move the King, it is stalemate straight away!

TEST 4

(Solutions at end of book)

Values of the pieces; notation—recording the moves; patterns of checkmate; drawn games.

Q.1. In the following position (Diagram 79) it is White to play. He has the opportunity of capturing Black's King's Bishop's Pawn. In this case play might well proceed thus:

1	Kt × P	R × Kt
2	B × R ch	K × B

If you are losing heavily and can see no hope of winning, look for opportunities of perpetual check or stalemate!

Would this Pawn capture and the exchanges which follow be to White's advantage, to Black's advantage or is the exchange equal?

79

White to play

White may capture Black's KB Pawn. Is it worth it?

Q.2. Look at the position in Diagram 80. Black, who has the move, is able to promote the Rook's Pawn next move. What form should this promotion take?

80

Black to play

Black may obtain a new Queen, but is this wise?

When considering an exchange or a Pawn promotion, calculate the merits of the position on the chessboard, as well as the table of relative values!

Q.3. Which White force is stronger, the two Rooks in Diagram 81, or the Queen in Diagram 82? Assume that it is White to play in each case.

81

82

Q.4. A question to test your skill in the understanding of chess notation. From the following position, play the moves recorded at side of Diagram 83. Check the final position you reach with the solution diagram shown on page 131, Diagram 184.

83

White to play

1 R—Kt1	Q—Kt5
2 Q×P ch	K×Q
3 B—R3 ch	K—B5
4 B—Kt5 ch	K×P
5 R(Kt1)—B1 mate	

Q.5. How may White force stalemate in the position shown in Diagram 84 in which Black has a great material advantage?

84

White to play

It is far better to give too much information than not enough when recording the moves of a game!

Q.6. Each of the following diagrams gives a position in which checkmate could be illustrated with the addition of a missing attacking piece. The identity of each missing piece is given. Indicate the squares on which each piece should stand. Where checkmate may be given from a choice of squares, indicate all such squares.

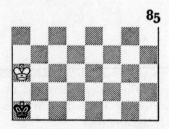

On which square should a WHITE ROOK be placed in order to show a position of checkmate?

On which square should a BLACK QUEEN be placed in order to show a position of checkmate?

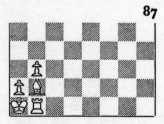

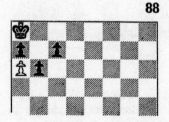

On which square should a BLACK KNIGHT be placed in order to show a position of checkmate?

On which square should a WHITE ROOK be placed in order to show a position of checkmate?

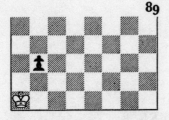

On which square should a BLACK QUEEN be placed in order to show a position of checkmate?

On which square should a BLACK ROOK be placed in order to show a position of checkmate?

Do not proceed to the next part of the book until you have correctly understood the principles involved in Questions 2 to 6.

CHAPTER 8

PAWNS IN END-GAME BATTLES

THAT stage of the game when only a few pieces and Pawns are left on the board, and where checkmate is either difficult or impossible to force because of the lack of the strength or the number of the pieces, is known as the 'End Game'.

In the end game, the deciding factor is often the attempt to promote a Pawn in order to give the attacking side the extra power needed for giving checkmate. Not all games reach the end-game stage, of course, as anyone who knows 'fool's mate' (1 P—KB4, P—K3; 2 P—KKt4, Q—R5 mate) or 'scholar's mate' (1 P—K4, P—K4; 2 B—B4, Kt—QB3; 3 Q—R5, Kt—B3; 4 Q×P mate) will tell you! As you become more experienced and proficient, however, more of your games are likely to reach the end-game stage, especially if you play experienced opponents.

The following sections offer a guide to the treatment of some of the more common situations you are likely to encounter in end-game battles.

Patterns of Strong and Weak Pawn Formations

One of the unique features of the move of the Pawn is, as we have already learned, its inability to move backwards. This means that an ill-considered Pawn advance cannot later be corrected. Pawn moves should, therefore, be made only after the most careful thought as to whether your present intention is going to be justified later in the game.

2	P—K4	P—K3	26
3	P—Q4	P—Q4	27
4	P—K5	P—QB4	28
5	Kt—QB3	Kt—QB3	29
6	B—B3	Q—Kt3	30
7	P×P	P×P	31
8	O—O	B—Q2	32
9	Kt—B3	KKt—K2	33
10	Kt×Kt	Kt×QP	34
11	Kt—Kt5	Q×Kt	35
12	R—K1	Q×KP	36
13	Q—B3	Q—Kt1	37
14	B×Kt	Kt—Kt3	38
15	B—B4	RP×B	39
16	Kt—B7ch	Q—Q1	40
17	Kt×QPch	K—K2	41
8	Kt—B7ch	K—K1	42
	Q—R3ch	K—K2	43
	Q—B3ch	K—B3	44
	—B5ch	K—K2	45
	Kt5 mate	K—B3	46
			47

4. A page from a scorebook showing the moves of a complete game. At the top of the sheet there is space for players' names, particulars of the event concerned, place, date, etc. On the reverse side of each scoresheet there is usually a diagram of a chessboard so that the position of an unfinished game may be recorded. When recording a position in this way, the initial letters of the pieces are written in the squares, the black pieces being ringed to avoid confusion.

5. Two examples of travelling chess sets. The set on the *right* folds up like a wallet, the pieces being magnetised. The other set (*below*) is of the more common peg-in variety, with a hole in the centre of each square to take the piece. Both kinds of chess sets have the advantage that they can be put away whilst a game is still in progress, without having to disturb the pieces.

(i) *Some Strong Pawn Situations*

91

92

Self-supporting Pawns. These two Pawns support each other against attack by the lone King, for if the King captures the rear Pawn (Q5), the other Pawn safely queens.

Self-supporting Pawns. If, in this position, White, having the move, plays 1 P—K6 the Black King cannot capture the other Pawn, without allowing the King's Pawn to queen.

In both of these examples, White would simply bring his King over to the Pawns and shepherd one (or both) to the eighth rank, with an easy win.

93

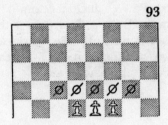

94

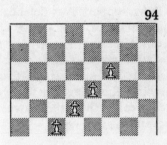

Pawn Barrier. These adjacent Pawns form a barrier of attack against the squares marked ∅. Should one of the Pawns be attacked in this kind of position, it is sometimes possible for it to be protected by advancing it one square forward.

Pawn Chain. Each of these Pawns, except the rear one, is protected by the Pawn behind it.

65

95

This is an example of an advanced passed Pawn, which, for the moment, is blocked by an enemy piece. Although halted, the Pawn is likely to be a serious threat to the opposing side, which has had to assign a blocking piece in order to prevent queening.

(ii) *Some Pawn Weaknesses*

96   **97**

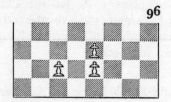

Doubled and Isolated Pawns. All these Pawns are weak, for none has Pawn support. Any defence for them, therefore, has to be with pieces. The two Pawns on the King's file are known as doubled Pawns. It is clear that the trio of Pawns in this diagram are very much weaker than the Pawns in Diagrams 93 and 94.

Backward Pawn. The white Pawn on Kt2 is known as a backward Pawn, since it cannot be supported by a Pawn on either adjacent file. If the backward Pawn advances, it may be captured by the black Pawn.

If you are in danger of running out of sufficient material with which to force checkmate, make sure you are left with at least one safe Pawn, so that queening may fill the gap!

98

White to play

99

Black to play

Pawn Breakthrough

1 P—Kt6 RP×P
2 P—B6!

If now 2 ..., P(Kt2)×P; 3 P—R6 and on to queen.

If after 1 P—Kt6, Black replies 1 ..., BP×P, there follows 2 P—R6, and if 2 ..., P(Kt2)×P; 3 P—B6, etc.

White queens first because his Pawns are farther advanced than those of Black.

Pawn Majority

Black may force a Pawn through, by:

1 ... P—Kt6

If now 2 P×P, there follows: 2 ..., P×P and on to queen.

If instead 2 P—R3, 2 ..., P—Kt7, etc.

Alternatively Black may wish to press home on the Rook's file.

1 ... P—R6

Followed by 2 ..., P—Kt6 and after 3 P×P, P—R7 and so on. In this variation White is allowed to retain the Pawn, but Black will queen first.

Practice

Set up the Pawn patterns illustrated, on a chessboard, and play through the variations given. Incorporate the patterns in invented complete positions and experiment with the strengths or weaknesses concerned. As well as using the patterns illustrated, vary them, so long as you retain the principles involved.

In the games you play, sustain your strong Pawn formations and exploit weaknesses in your opponent's Pawn defences, as demonstrated.

King and Pawn Against King
The Pawn Chase—How Counting May Help to Calculate the Chances of Promoting a Pawn

If in the position shown in Diagram 100 below, you are in the happy position of being Black, you clearly have an easy win, for whatever White does, he is unable to stop your Pawn from queening. The position in Diagram 101 is not so clear, however. Can you see, at a glance, whether Black may also safely queen this Pawn?

100

Black to play

101

Black to play

Easy to see the Pawn may queen.   Can White capture this Pawn?

There is a simple method of calculating whether a Pawn may queen in situations like these, where no piece other than the opposing King may hinder the chase.

If, with the Pawn to move, *it may reach the queening square in fewer moves than the opposing King, the Pawn may safely queen. If not, the Pawn may be captured.*

Look again at Diagram 101. It is Black to play, and since the Pawn moves first, the counting sequence may be introduced. It needs four moves for the Pawn to reach the queening square. Now count the moves needed for the white King to reach the same square—the King needs five moves. Since the Pawn is able to reach the queening square in fewer moves than the opposing King, the Pawn may queen safely. (Try the Pawn chase for yourself, on the chessboard, and prove the counting rule.)

68

Should it have been White to play in the position shown in Diagram 101 we assume a move of the King to Q4. Now we can again implement our counting rule.

The Pawn needs four moves to reach the queening square, and the white King also needs four moves. The situation is now essentially different, for the Pawn is unable to reach the queening square in fewer moves than the opposing King. The Pawn will be captured, on queening, and the result is a draw.

Practice

Invent Pawn chase situations until facility is gained in the counting method. If the Pawn is not to be protected by its King, the latter may, for the purposes of these exercises, be removed from the board. Use Pawns on various parts of the board, and include chases which start with the Pawns on their starting squares. The long Pawn chases are a little more difficult to calculate than short ones!

The Opposition

Look at the following position in which the two Kings face each other across the rank.

102

Neither King may, at present, move to the squares marked ϕ because of the rule of check.

In positions with King and Pawn v. King, the lone Pawn is your only hope of winning—guard it tenaciously!

Suppose both Kings wished to be the first to advance to the rank separating them, which one would be successful? The answer to the question depends on whose turn it is to move. Suppose it is White to play, then 1 K—K5, K—B3; and Black has reached the intervening rank first. Or 1 K—B5, K—K3; and again Black arrives first at the rank which separates them. In either case the strange fact emerges that Black is successful in reaching the rank separating them first, despite the fact that White moved first from the facing position.

Now consider the position (Diagram 102) as if it were Black to move: 1 ... K—B2; 2 K—K6, and White advances to the intervening rank first. Or 1 ... K—K2; 2 K—B6. We see that with Black to move, it is White who succeeds in winning the short race to the separating rank.

In the kind of situation illustrated in Diagram 102, therefore, the side having the move may be forced to give ground. The side which is able to advance the King in the way described is said to have the 'opposition'. Just how important the opposition is will be shown in the King and Pawn examples which follow.

In endings with King and single Pawn against King, in which the defending lone King is able to control the vital queening square, the side with the Pawn should advance the King ahead of the Pawn in its march up the board to the eighth rank. In a position in which a white Pawn is on Q2, a white King on Q4 (two squares ahead of the Pawn), and the black King on Black's Q3, White may safely queen the Pawn, whichever side has the move.

In the position in Diagram 103, White's King, ahead of the Pawn, is able to force a clear passage to the queening square, whichever side has the move.

103

An ideal position for the side with the Pawn, for whether it is White or Black to move, the white King and Pawn may co-operate in forcing the black King to give ground.

Consider the position first, as if it were White to play. Black has the opposition; but not for long.

White	Black
1 K—K6	K—K1

In this kind of ending, the defending King should always attempt to face the attacking King across the rank, in the way shown.

2 P—Q6

Gaining the opposition for White.

2 ...	K—Q1
3 P—Q7	K—B2
4 K—K7	

And White controls the queening square with 5 P—Q8 = Q to follow. Work out the similar winning pattern which arises from 1 K—B6, etc.

Now back to the position in Diagram 103, but with Black to play, White having the opposition:

1 ...	K—B1

White having the opposition, the black King has to give ground.

2 K—K7

The white King advances to control the queening square.

2 ...	K—B2
3 P—Q6 ch	K—B1
4 P—Q7 ch	

And queens next move. A similar pattern arises from the variation commencing 1 ... K—K1

The pattern of King and Pawn against King, shown in Diagram 103, wins for the side with the Pawn in all cases except when on the Rook's file. Look at the following position:

104

White to play

1 K—Kt6	K—Kt1
2 P—R6	K—R1
3 P—R7 stalemate	

The same result, a draw, arises with Black to play in the position shown in Diagram 104, e.g.

White	Black
1 ...	K—Kt1
2 K—Kt6	K—R1
3 P—R6	K—Kt1
4 P—R7 ch	K—R1
5 K—R6 stalemate	

With best play on both sides, the defending King, by moving backwards and forwards between R1 and Kt1, is able to retain control of the queening square. Experiment with the position shown in Diagram 104, and confirm that a draw results from all variations, whichever side has the move.

In the position shown in Diagram 105, although White wins by P 1—Q7 if it is White to play, Black, with the move, may force a draw.

105

Black to play

Will White be able to promote the Pawn?

1 ...	K—B1!

The defending King faces the attacking King across the rank.

2 P—Q7 ch	K—Q1

If now 3 K—Q6 stalemate, or the white King moves away from the defence of the Pawn, which will then be captured. In either case a draw results.

In endings with King and Pawn against King, the side with the Pawn should endeavour to advance the King ahead of the Pawn, when marching it up the board towards the queening square.

Practice

Set up positions in which the two Kings directly face each other across either rank or file, and experiment to find which side may first reach the rank or file separating them.

Set up the position illustrated in Diagram 103 again, but *without the Pawn*. Confirm by experiment that, with White to play (Black having the opposition), because of the absence of the Pawn, White may *not* now be able to control queening square Q8.

Invent positions with only Kings and Pawns, in which possession of the opposition is vital to the victory of the winning side.

Set up a position with a white King on K4, white Pawn on K5 and black King on K1. Confirm that, with correct play on both sides, a draw results, whichever side has the move, because in the approach towards the queening square, the Pawn has been advanced in front of the white King.

Place a white Pawn on QR6, white King on QR8 and black King on QB1. With White or Black to play, ensure that Black may prevent the Pawn from queening.

King, Rook and Pawn Against King and Rook

Because of its file attacking action, a Rook on the first rank is particularly effective in support of a Pawn of the same side, advancing in front of it towards the eighth rank. Rooks are commonly used to protect Pawns in the end game. In the end game, when some or all of the minor pieces have been exchanged off the board, the Rooks are less vulnerable to harassing attacks and may advance more freely from the first rank. It is then that the Rook comes into its own as the natural guardian of the passed Pawn.

The pattern in Diagram 106 is familiar to chess players of all strengths.

When two Kings face each other across the rank or file, and a King move must be made, assuming that there is no interference from other pieces, the side not having the move enjoys the opposition. The side having the move may be forced to give ground!

The white Rook is behind the Pawn. Compare the freedom of the white Rook, which may move anywhere along the file as far as Q6 and still protect the Pawn, with that of the black Rook, which dare not move at all because of the queening threat of White's Pawn.

Now look at the following position in which White's Rook and Pawn are on the same squares as those in Diagram 106. The two Kings have been added.

107

Although Black would have preferred his Rook to be at Q1 in order to block the queening action of the Pawn, the white King's attack on this square prevents its safe occupation by the Rook.

White to play

In this position White wins either with a new Queen, by P—Q8 = Q ch., or, should Black give up his Rook for the new Queen, with King and Rook against King.

In Diagram 108 the white Rook, instead of being behind the Pawn, is in front of it.

108

White to play

If the white Rook vacates Q8, the Pawn will be captured by the black Rook. If the white King moves over to the Pawn, in order to take over its protection, thus freeing White's Rook from its imprisonment at Q8, Black will simply keep checking.

Because of the awkward position of the white Rook, the game may be drawn, despite the fact that the Pawn is on the seventh rank.

If, in the position shown in Diagram 108, the black King were on KKt3, instead of KKt2, White, by means of a check, would be able to queen his Pawn, e.g.:

White	Black
1 R—KKt8 ch	K—B2
2 P—Q8 = Q	

If now 2 ... R×Q; 3 R×R.

See if you can find other squares of possible occupation by the black King, which give White similar opportunities of a winning check.

Not all Rook and Pawn endings are as straightforward as these examples, but the principle of supporting your advancing Pawn *with the Rook behind it*, is fundamental.

King and Rook Against King and Two Pawns

In most cases, a mere two Pawns are no match for the powerful Rook. Two isolated or even linked Pawns will usually be easy prey for the Rook. It is possible, however, for two connected Pawns to win against the Rook, if the Pawns have advanced to the sixth rank.

The Rook gives best protection from behind the passed Pawn!

109

White to play

Here, the two Pawns are extremely strong. Had they not been so far advanced, Black, could with little difficulty, have captured them both.

White			Black	
1 P—K7	R×P	or	1 P—Q7	R—Q3
2 P—K8 = Q			2 P—K7	R×P
			3 P—K8 = Q	

	or	1 P—Q7	R—K8
		2 P—Q8 = Q	R×P

King and Minor Piece in the End Game

Since the King and a minor piece cannot checkmate the lone King, clearly the importance of the minor piece in endings with minor pieces and one or two Pawns, lies in the ability to use the piece either to force or foil Pawn promotion.

In the following position White may force a draw by 1 Kt—Q2, *blocking the Queen's Pawn and attacking the Bishop's Pawn's queening square.* Now the white King may advance on the Pawns and capture them, for the black King is too remote to interfere. Note that 1 Kt—K3, attacking both Pawns' queening squares would not do, since Black would reply 1 ... P—Q7, followed either by 2 ... P—Q8 = Q ch. or 2 ... P—B8 = Q. White may capture the first Pawn to queen, but not the other one!

76

110

White to play

The white Knight may blockade the Queen's Pawn and at the same time attack the queening square of the Bishop's Pawn.

The position shown in Diagram 111 is another example of how a minor piece, this time a Bishop, may be used to good advantage:

111

Black to play

1 ...   B—K3

Attacking the queening square of the Knight's Pawn. Should the Knight's Pawn now queen, it may be captured by the Bishop. If the other Pawn advances, the black King may capture it. Once Black has captured the Queen's Pawn, leaving the Bishop on K3 to control KKt1, the black King may shepherd one or both of the self-supporting Pawns to queen.

King and Queen Against King and Pawn

There follow two examples of how the King and lone Pawn may draw.

Just as in most examples of Rook against one or two Pawns, the Rook usually wins, so, obviously, will a Queen usually succeed against one or two Pawns. It is, however, possible for a single Pawn, with only King support, to draw against the King and Queen. The positions which follow are important and instructive in underlining the power of the advanced passed Pawn, as well as in illustrating once again, examples of how the losing side may sometimes snatch the 'triumph' of stalemate from seemingly certain disaster:

77

112

1 K—R8   Q—B3 or Q1 ch
2 K—Kt8 or Kt7

And so on. The white King simply keeps as close to QR8 as he can. Black, for his part, must keep checking in order to stop the Pawn's promotion. With careful play on both sides, the ending will be drawn.

113

1 K—R8

If now 1 . . . Q × P, White is stalemated. Since Black is unable to capture the Pawn without giving stalemate, the game is drawn.

Practice

Set up Pawn battle patterns similar to those on pages 65–78 and get the 'feel' of the various situations they represent. Set up positions where you are able to exercise possibilities of attack and defence.

In the positions you invent, incorporate, where appropriate, the use of both check and checkmate.

> **When considering ways of capturing an advanced passed Pawn, remember that a Pawn is unable to attack a piece which is behind it!**

When setting up practice positions of attack, remember the following principles:

King, Rook and Pawn against King and Rook. Keep the protecting Rook behind the Pawn. If your opponent stations a Rook on the queening square of the Pawn, try and drive it off with your King.

If, for some reason, your Rook has to defend the Pawn from in front of it, try and check with the Rook, as described on page 75, to retrieve the situation.

In endings with King and Queen against a King and an advanced passed Pawn, always bear in mind the possibilities of stalemate.

If you have King and minor pieces against a King and a Pawn about to queen, safely be prepared to give up a minor piece for the new Queen.

When considering these practice positions from the point of view of the defender, attempt to *prevent* the attacking side from applying the correct attacking principles outlined!

'Pity about that game. So concerned with my own attack I forgot all about my opponent's . . . .'

TEST 5

(Solutions at end of book)

Endings with Kings and Pawns, with or without the participation of other pieces, in which Pawn promotion is vital to the victory of the winning side; the opposition; strong and weak Pawn situations.

114

White to play

115

White to play

Q.1. How may White best proceed?

Q.2. Assuming no interference by other pieces, is it possible for White to force a passed Pawn through?

116

White to play

117

Black to play

Q.3. May Black safely queen this pawn?

Q.4. Will White be able to promote the Pawn?

6. Play in progress at the Stevenson Memorial Tournament held at the Bognor International Congress.

7. Champion v. The Rest! Former world champion Vassily Smyslov of the U.S.S.R. demonstrating his virtuosity in the course of a simultaneous display held at Vienna in 1957. It is not surprising that occasionally an 'unknown' comes forward to beat the Master under these conditions.

118

Black to play

Q.5. Will this position end in a draw, or win for White?

Q.6. Now assume it is White to play in the position shown in Diagram 118. What then?

119

120

Black to play

Q.7. Consider this position from the point of view of both sides having the first move:

    (i) White to play;

    (ii) Black to play.

Q.8. Is this a win for Black or is White able to force a draw?

81

6

121   122

White to play   Black to play

Q.9. White to play: can he force a win?

Q.10. Black to play: can he save the game?

Do not proceed to the next part of the book until you have correctly understood the principles involved in all the questions in this test.

CHAPTER 9

THE MIDDLE GAME

Space, Open Lines and Tactical Combinations

IN the previous section, you have seen examples of winning end-game positions and some weaknesses to avoid. The time to start thinking about achieving a strong end-game situation is not when the end game is upon you, but in the commencing stages of the game. Sound generalship in the early stages of a complex battle lies not in regarding every little skirmish as a self-contained unit, but as a part of a larger pattern of events, in which many considerations of attack and defence have constantly to be borne in mind.

One feature of battle, vital to chess players and generals alike, is the importance of space and lines of communication, through which to manœuvre forces rapidly. In the end game, with many pieces exchanged, space for manœuvrability is often generously afforded. In the earlier stages of the game, however, the creation and exploitation of space and open lines requires careful preparation.

If you are not constantly to be restricted by cramped situations in the middle game, you should bear in mind the need for easy mobility right from the start of the game.

The positions in Diagrams 123 and 125 show how space and un-obstructed lines may be used to advantage by the players who have deployed their forces well.

123

Black to play

Note the square attacking power of Black's Rooks along the Queen's file and King's Rook's file, and the strong outlook enjoyed by the black Bishop at QKt2, along the long white square diagonal. Most of White's pieces, on the other hand, are poorly placed.

White	Black
1 ...	Kt—Kt5 ch!

White's King's Rook's Pawn may not capture the Knight, for this would be putting White into check by the black Queen.

| 2 K—Kt1 | |

Now White's King has moved out of line with Black's Queen.

| 2 ... | Q×KBP ch |
| 3 K—R1 | Q×R mate |

Black's first step in the above attack incorporates the following basic form:

124

The white Pawn on KR3 is as good as 'pinned' to its square.

Here is another position in which several well-positioned pieces combine together in attack:

84

125

White to play

Black's unguarded Queen is on the same rank as the white Queen, with only the white Bishop (Q3) between them. Can you see any way in which White may take advantage of this factor?

1 Kt×B!

If now 1 ... P×Kt, White may use the Bishop which intervenes between the two Queens, in order to give check, by 2 B—Kt6. After Black relieves the check, White wins the black Queen with 3 Q×Q. Black may, of course, avoid losing the Queen by safeguarding it on his first move, instead of 1 ... P×Kt, but must, in any event, lose a piece.

In the kind of position in Diagram 125, White would cast around for a way of giving check with the piece which divided the two Queens. Such a way not being immediately available, a forcing introductory move (in the example just shown it was 1 Kt×B) should be sought.

The idea in Diagram 126 was at the heart of White's attack.

126

White threatens to uncover an attack on the black Queen by moving the Bishop, giving check.

Patterns of Tactical Devices

There follow some more patterns of tactical ideas which are commonly used to win games. To illustrate the themes more clearly, we have limited the diagram material used to the basic essentials.

Open lines for Queens, Rooks and Bishops!

It is not possible to show every form of tactical device here. The examples which follow are presented in the hope, not only that you will find them practically instructive, but also that you will be encouraged to invent others like them.

127

Discovered attack.

128

Discovered check.

An example with a motif similar to that illustrated in Diagram 126. Kt—KB7 ch. uncovers an attack on the black Queen.

Similar to the discovered attack example, except the black King and Queen have been reversed, but *uncovering check* this time. It is common practice to record the fact that a move is a discovered check, as shown: Kt—B7 *dis. ch.*

129

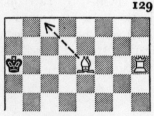

Double check.

130

The Pin.

A most lethal tactical device, which not only gives check by the piece uncovered in the attack, but also by the piece which does the uncovering. The only way of relieving a double check is to move the King, for you cannot get out of double check by blocking the attack. Notice how the notation record includes a reference to the double check: B—QB8 *db. ch.*

Black must give up the Queen, which is pinned to the file on which it stands. To move the Queen away from the King's file would be to put Black into check; such a move would be illegal.

131

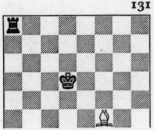

Skewer.

132

Overworked Piece.

The Bishop strikes at the black King, behind which lies the Rook. The King must move out of check, after which White may capture the Rook. In effect, the Bishop strikes at the Rook, *through* the square on which the black King stands.

White to play. Black's Queen protects not only the Knight's Pawn, but the Rook on the first rank as well.

  1 R×R ch   Q×R

  2 Q×P mate

In fulfilling one role, the Queen was unable to carry out the other!

133

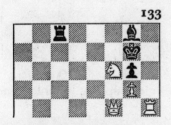

Clearance Sacrifice.

134

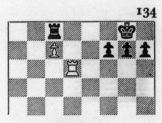

Queening.

White to play. The Knight stands in the way of White's Q—B6 mate. So:

  1 Kt—K8 ch   R×Kt

  2 Q—B6 mate

White to play. White's strong Pawn needs no protection:

  1 R—Q8 ch   R×R

  2 P×R = Q or R mate

135

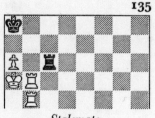

Stalemate.

Black to play:

1 ...   R × P ch
2 K × R stalemate

136

Knight Fork.

Black to play. Attack by a Knight on two or more pieces at once. In this position Black must relieve the check, allowing the capture of the Queen next move.

137

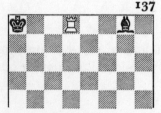

Rook fork.

Attack by Rook on two or more pieces at once. Black must get out of check, after which the Bishop is captured.

138   139

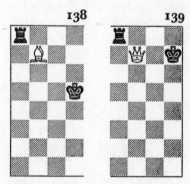

Bishop fork.   Queen fork.
More examples of double attack.

Favourable Conditions for Winning Tactical Advantage

Some tactical ideas win in their own right, regardless of the general state of mobility of the winning side. In the great majority of cases, however, successful tactical advantages, often in the form of *a series of forced moves*, arise from forces strongly placed with fluid mobility.

Be prepared to give up material if you gain an advantage as a result!

88

Search for tactical ideas from weak situations by all means, but from positions of strength, you will find your opportunities multiply.

The following checkmate example shows a twofold tactical attack, the first stage of which involves a sacrifice. It illustrates the possibilities which may arise from the exploitation of a simple theme, under conditions of power (pieces posted to good advantage) and mobility (open lines and useful manœuvring space).

140

White to play

White, in contemplating this position in which he has previously given up a Knight, notices that he could play Q—Q8 mate, if it were not for his Bishop on Q2. One way of removing the Bishop would be to move it to, say, B3, Kt4, etc., but this would give Black time to block the threatened checkmate. White finds that he has not been wasting his time in his contemplations, for the idea of moving the Bishop has developed to provide *another* pattern of forced checkmate!

1 Q—Q8 ch!	K × Q
2 B—Kt5 db. ch	K—K1
3 R—Q8 mate	

The next example (Diagram 141) involves a winning method not classified in the basic patterns.

141

Black to play

The white Bishop at Q4 is doubly attacked and doubly defended.

If Black plays 1 ... Kt×B; 2 R×Kt, R×R; 3 Q×R, the exchange is equal. By means of removing one of the pieces guarding the Bishop, however, Black is able to win a piece:

1 ...   Q×Q

One of the guards is removed.

2 P×Q   Kt×B

and Black is a piece up.

The position in Diagram 142 shows how it is possible for one tactical device to be used to defeat another.

142

Black to play

Black has pinned the white Knight at KB3 by the Bishop. He decides to attack the pinned piece a second time.

1 ...   Kt—Q5

2 B×P ch! (*see* Diagram 143)

143

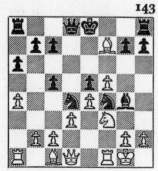

White appears to be giving up a Bishop. Is this a blunder?

If now:

2 ...   K×B

3 Kt×P ch   King moves

4 Kt×B

90

White has not only won two Pawns, but prevented Black from castling!

Remember there are numerous other tactical devices which do not lend themselves to the more common classifications, but which are just as effective as those illustrated. If the winning tactical plan does not emerge of its own accord, then try and create it! And when you have created it, try to improve upon it, before putting it into effect.

Two short games follow, showing tactical considerations arising from well-placed forces working in harmony.

The first game was won by the great Paul Morphy, who took the chess world by storm over a hundred years ago. He won this game (at the age of twelve!) against his father:

Game 2. Played at New Orleans, 1849.

White	Black
PAUL MORPHY	ALONZO MORPHY
1 P—K4	P—K4
2 Kt—KB3	Kt—QB3
3 B—B4	B—B4
4 P—QKt4	B × KtP
5 P—B3	

This move, which opens up the diagonal Q1–QR4 for possible use by the Queen, explains the sacrifice of the Pawn on White's 4th move.

5 ...	B—B4
6 P—Q4	P × P
7 P × P	B—Kt3
8 O—O	Kt—R4
9 B—Q3	P—Q4?

This is a poor move because although it releases the Queen's Bishop, it allows White to open up the King's file, at the other end of which is Black's *uncastled* King. 9 ... P—Q3, releasing the Bishop just the same, would have been much better.

10 P × P	Q × P
11 B—R3	B—K3
12 Kt—B3	

Experiment, and create your own short cuts to victory!

This move, which develops a piece with an attack against another piece, is a useful time-saver, for in moving the Queen away from the attack, Black is, for the moment, prevented from continuing with his mobilisation.

| 12 ... | Q—Q2 |

13 P—Q5 (*See* Diagram 144)

144

Position after 13 P—Q5

Compare the square attacking power of the two sides. Black still has to develop his King's Knight and has not yet castled. Not content with his advantage White now offers up his Queen's Pawn, to improve his lot still more.

13 ...	B×QP
14 Kt×B	Q×Kt
15 B—Kt5 ch	

A winning discovered attack on the black Queen, sacrificing the Bishop, in order to clear the Queen's file.

| 15 ... | Q×B |
| 16 R—K1 ch | Kt—K2 |

The Knight moves on to a square doubly attacked, but defended only by the King.

17 R—Kt1	Q—R3
18 R×Kt ch	K—B1
19 Q—Q5	

This explains White's 17th move, driving the black Queen away, for if the black Queen had remained on QKt4, the present move by White would not have been possible.

19 ...	Q—B5
20 R×KBP db. ch	K—Kt1
21 R—B8 db. checkmate (*See* Diagram 145)	

145

Final position after
21 R—B8 mate

Two lethal double checks bring an end to Black's resistance. White mobilised *all* his major and minor pieces; Black, on the other hand, concluded the game, not having developed either Rook, and having been prevented from castling.

The next game won the *Liverpool Daily Post* Brilliancy Cup in the Under-fifteen Championship at the 1966 Liverpool Junior Easter Congress:

Game 3.

White	Black
R. BAILEY	P. H. MCKEOWN
1 P—Q4	Kt—KB3
2 P—QB4	P—K3
3 Kt—QB3	B—Kt5

Pinning the white Knight against the Queen.

4 P—K3	B × Kt ch
5 P × B	P—QKt3
6 B—R3	B—Kt2
7 R—Kt1	P—Q3
8 P—B3	O—O
9 B—Q3	R—K1
10 Kt—K2	QKt—Q2
11 O—O	P—B4
12 P—K4	Q—B2

See Diagram 146.

146

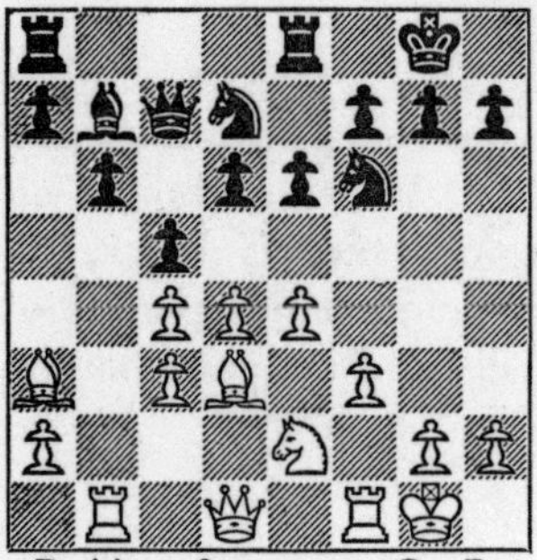

Both sides prepare to come to grips. White's fourth rank Pawn barrier is very strong.

Position after 12 ... Q—B2

White	Black
13 Q—B2	P—QR3
14 P—B4	P—K4
15 BP × P	QP × P
16 P—Q5	

This is now a passed Pawn.

| 16 ... | Q—Q3 |

Blocking the passed Pawn.

| 17 Kt—Kt3 | P—Kt3 |

This move, weakening as it does, the castled King's defences, is designed to prevent White's Kt—B5, which would attack the black Queen as well as the castled King's position.

18 B—B1

Since this Bishop does not seem to have much scope at R3, White brings it back to its starting square. Diagonal QB1—R6 looks more promising for this piece.

18 ...	K—Kt2
19 Q—Q2	Kt—KKt1
20 Q—Kt5	K—R1
21 R × BP	R—KB1
22 Kt—B5	

94

The black Queen is attacked, despite the efforts made to prevent this! Although it is legally possible for the black King's Knight's Pawn to capture the Knight, the Pawn is virtually pinned because of the threat of 23 Q—Kt7 mate which would follow. *See* Diagram 147.

147

Position after 22 Kt—B5

White has launched a violent attack against the black King, using Queen, Rook and Knight, with Queen's Bishop in support.

White	Black
22 ...	Q—B2

In hiding itself from White's attack, Black's Queen has to desert the harassed King.

    23 R×RP ch

A sacrifice to draw the King out into the open.

23 ...	K×R
24 Q—R4 ch	Kt—R3
25 Q×Kt ch	K—Kt1
26 Q—Kt7 mate	

See Diagram 148.

148

Final position after
26 Q—Kt7 mate

The sacrifice on White's 23rd move was justified! Looking back at White's 22nd move, you will now see that this was really a double attack by the Knight, against the black Queen and square KKt7. Square KKt7 is the one on which the white Queen has given checkmate!

Practice

Set up tactical device basic patterns similar to those on pages 86–88.

Set up and play over tactical device situations in complete positions, and include examples which lead to checkmate. Include positions which involve a *forcing first move* leading to a winning tactical device on the second move.

In creating these positions, remember that most pieces enjoy the maximum square attacking strength in or near the centre of the board and that all pieces need *room to move*!

If some of the winning practice positions you invent include examples of devices of your own creation, so much the better!

'How on earth did I manage to forget that my Queen was under attack? Never mind, I'll remember to take more care of it next time . . . .'

TEST 6
(Solutions at end of book)

Testing use of space, open lines and tactical devices.

The following examples include tactical methods already discussed as well as one we have not classified:

149

Q.1. How may White force checkmate with Queen aided by Pawn?

White to play

150

Black to play

Q.2. We have stated earlier that one way of getting out of attack is by blocking the attack with one of your own pieces. How is Black able to win a valuable piece by *blocking part of the defence of the enemy King*?

151

White to play

Q.3. How may White force checkmate? The solution involves a double check?

152

Black to play

Q.4. How may Black win material as a result of a discovered attack?

153

White to play

Q.5. How may White win material by means of a Knight fork?

154

White to play

Q.6. White wins material with the help of a pin. How may this be achieved?

Do not proceed to the next part of the book until you have correctly understood the principles involved in all the questions in this test.

98

CHAPTER 10

THE OPENING

Pieces and the Centre

THE diagrams which follow show the varying power of the pieces when situated in different parts of the chessboard, and underline, in some detail, the reasons for this fluctuating value.

155

The white Bishop on centre square Q5 commands thirteen squares. The Bishop on corner square QR1 commands only seven squares.

In Diagram 156 the attacking power of the Bishop is shown, as from every square of the board. In Diagrams 157 to 159 are shown the square attacking power of the other pieces.

Square attacking power of the Bishop

156

7	7	7	7	7	7	7	7
7	9	9	9	9	9	9	7
7	9	11	11	11	11	9	7
7	9	11	13	13	11	9	7
7	9	11	13	13	11	9	7
7	9	11	11	11	11	9	7
7	9	9	9	9	9	9	7
7	7	7	7	7	7	7	7

The Bishop enjoys greatest power when situated on one of the four centre squares, from which it attacks thirteen squares. It is least powerful when placed at the side of the board.

Square attacking power of the Knight

157

2	3	4	4	4	4	3	2
3	4	6	6	6	6	4	3
4	6	8	8	8	8	6	4
4	6	8	8	8	8	6	4
4	6	8	8	8	8	6	4
4	6	8	8	8	8	6	4
3	4	6	6	6	6	4	3
2	3	4	4	4	4	3	2

The Knight enjoys the most power when situated in or near the centre. The Knight is least powerful when placed in the corner of the board.

Square attacking power of the Rook

158

14	14	14	14	14	14	14	14
14	14	14	14	14	14	14	14
14	14	14	14	14	14	14	14
14	14	14	14	14	14	14	14
14	14	14	14	14	14	14	14
14	14	14	14	14	14	14	14
14	14	14	14	14	14	14	14
14	14	14	14	14	14	14	14

The Rook, unlike other pieces, attacks the same number of squares on whichever square it is situated.

Square attacking power of the Queen

159

21	21	21	21	21	21	21	21
21	23	23	23	23	23	23	21
21	23	25	25	25	25	23	21
21	23	25	27	27	25	23	21
21	23	25	27	27	25	23	21
21	23	25	25	25	25	23	21
21	23	23	23	23	23	23	21
21	21	21	21	21	21	21	21

The Queen has most power when positioned on one of the four centre squares. It is least powerful at the side of the board.

Pawns and the Centre

Pawns, too, have an important role in the centre. The advance of the King's Pawn and Queen's Pawn to the fourth rank not only opens up lines of movement for Queen and Bishops, but forms a barrier of attack against squares QB5, Q5, K5 and KB5.

160

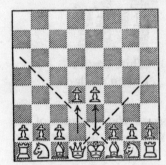

White's King's Pawn and Queen's Pawn form a barrier of attack against Black's fourth rank squares as indicated. Such a barrier helps to deprive the enemy of the occupation of these important squares.

In these two moves, White has achieved the following:

    (i) released Queen and both Bishops;

    (ii) stopped the safe occupation by Black of four squares in and near the centre.

Pawn Protection of the Castled King

If it is often important for centre file Pawns to be advanced early in the game, it is equally vital that the Pawns in front of the castled King be advanced only if and when it is absolutely necessary. A row of unmoved Pawns in front of the castled position creates a strong barrier of attack against the squares immediately ahead, whilst Pawns advanced in front of the castled King at the beginning of the game may provide weaknesses which invite disaster.

The centre of the chessboard is valuable—do not give it up to the enemy without a struggle!

Unmoved Pawns in front of the castled King present the following patterns:

161

White castles
King's side

162

White castles
Queen's side

In the case of the position shown in Diagram 162, because of the lack of protection of the Queen's Rook's Pawn, it is sometimes found desirable to move the King to Kt1, in order to remedy the weakness. In other respects both castled positions may be regarded as strong, since there are no gaps through which enemy pieces may readily infiltrate.

The following two castled positions represent fairly common situations and are usually found to be satisfactory:

163

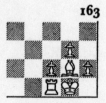

164

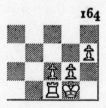

Fairly strong, provided the Bishop concerned is not exchanged or captured. The danger of playing this kind of Pawn formation without the Bishop is demonstrated in Game No. 3, page 93. When a Bishop is developed at Kt2 in this way, it is known as a *fianchetto*.

Fairly strong, but owing to the gap created in the Pawn defence, not so strong as in Diagram 161.

165

166

Both of the above castled positions (Diagrams 165 and 166) must be regarded as very unsafe defensively, because of the many gaps created in the Pawn pattern.

It is often found desirable, in later stages of a game, to advance into enemy territory the Pawn which stands in front of the castled Rook. This need not prove a weakness; indeed, it may be the spearhead of a winning attack, provided the remaining defences of the castled King are adequate to meet requirements against possible attack from the other side. Sometimes several, if not all, of the Pawns protecting the castled King, may be advanced against the opposing side's castled position, if the pressure so built-up leaves the enemy no time to launch an effective counter-attack.

CHAPTER 11

GUIDE TO MOBILISATION

IF you re-examine the winning situations in the middle game section, you will find, in every case, that the victorious side enjoyed superior command of space in and around the centre of the board. This link between control of the centre and successful conclusion, underlines the fundamental importance of developing your pieces centrally, where their square-attacking power is greatest.

The middle part of the chessboard is important, also, because it is an area from which pieces may best deal with needs of attack and defence in any part of the board. It is little wonder, then, that occupation of the centre, either immediately or ultimately, is an aim common to all good chess players.

Although games may be won without developing your pieces to squares of maximum hitting power—indeed there will be numerous occasions when a piece is best developed at a square other than in or near the centre—it is clear that if you wish to exploit your opportunities to the full, your pieces must usually be placed in strong square-attacking positions, and once there, used to good advantage.

Think of the chessboard as a battlefield in which the centre is a hill! Just as in battle the military commander would attempt to occupy the hill and deny it to the enemy, so in chess, the occupation of the centre is the prize which both sides strive to win and hold, in the early stages of the struggle.

In the starting position, the only pieces able to move are the Pawns and Knights. The task of each player to mobilise his forces to the full is both vital and urgent. Time wasted by using up several moves to get a piece to a square which need have taken only one or two moves, is tantamount to giving aid to the enemy; if this sort of neglect happens too often, the survival of the backward developer is likely to be on a precarious basis!

Mobilise in as few moves as possible—the quicker you prepare, the quicker you can attack!

The following advice may be of assistance in mobilising your forces to the best advantage:

1. In the starting position, the King's Pawn and Queen's Pawn represent doors which restrict the free action of the Queen and Bishops. If you are able to advance the King's Pawn and Queen's Pawn in the first few moves of the game, thereby freeing Queen and both Bishops, you will have made a good start.

2. When developing your minor pieces, move a Knight first, followed either by the other Knight or a Bishop. The reason for this is that it is not always immediately clear which squares of development are best for the Bishops, and moving a Knight out first gives you more time to consider the best squares to which the Bishops may be posted.

3. Since the advance of the centre file Pawns is likely to expose the unmoved King to dangers of attack, it is invariably advantageous to castle early in the game. Castling tucks the King away to comparative safety and develops a Rook towards the centre files. Although it is more common to castle King's side, there are occasions when Queen's side castling meets the needs of correct opening play.

4. Do not, as a rule, advance your Queen or Rooks early in the game, without the utmost vigilance. Such advances made whilst most of the enemy minor pieces and Pawns are still on the board, put the major pieces in danger, since they are liable to be the harassed targets of enemy development.

5. It is sometimes worthwhile to give up a Pawn in the opening, in return for quicker development. Such an opening sacrifice is known as a gambit. If you give up a Pawn, or even a more valuable piece, for this reason, and are able to build up a winning attack as a result, the sacrifice involved is clearly justified. Always make sure you obtain a good return for your gambit Pawn—the material given up is meant to be an investment, not a donation to the enemy!

6. There follow the opening moves of a game in which White develops his pieces rapidly to strong squares, whilst Black mobilises haphazardly and without thought for the coming battle:

White	Black
1 P—K4	

White occupies one of the four centre squares, at the same time attacking Q5 and KB5. Moreover, this move releases White's Queen and King's Bishop. A single move which does so much must be good!

| 1 ... | P—K3 |
| 2 P—Q4 | |

White occupies another centre square and releases the Queen's Bishop. With this, and his first move, White has now created a barrier of attack against squares QB5, Q5, K5 and KB5. White's development, only two moves old, has made excellent progress.

| 2 ... | P—Q3 |

Black, after two moves, has only two extra squares of movement open to his Bishops.

| 3 Kt—KB3 | |

This Knight, in moving towards the centre, attacks square K5 a second time, and supports the Queen's Pawn.

| 3 ... | B—K2 |
| 4 Kt—B3 | |

This attacks centre square Q5 a second time, and supports the King's Pawn.

| 4 ... | B—Q2 |
| 5 B—QB4 | |

More support for the centre. Now square Q5 is attacked for the third time.

| 5 ... | Kt—KR3 |

In developing the Knight to the side of the board, Black fails to take full advantage of the potential of the piece.

| 6 B—B4 | |

Square K5 is attacked for the third time.

6 ...   Kt—R3

7 O—O

The King is safely tucked away from the centre files along which the Pawns have advanced. Although such files are dangerous for the King, they are ideal for the castled Rook which now moves towards them.

7 ...   P—QB3

This move shuts in the Queen's Bishop.

8 Q—K2

The Queen moves from the back rank—but not too far! Now each white Rook supports the other.

8 ...   P—B3

Black's final move in this variation, in shutting in the King's Bishop, sets the seal on a cramped and ineffective development. *See* Diagram 167.

167

White has made an ideal start with his mobilisation. Black's pieces, in contrast, have a very poor outlook!

Position after 8 ... P—B3

The ideal position enjoyed by White in Diagram 167, is only possible if Black's opening moves are aimless. Two players of equal playing strength will clearly compete strongly for occupation of the centre. In the games you play, you will be fortunate indeed ever to find yourself in the happy situation achieved by White in the opening just described!

When making developing moves, do not shut in your own pieces. Imprison the enemy forces, by all means, but not your own!

Since opening advantage gained in the ways we have just been discussing may easily be sustained right through to final victory, consideration of the principles of opening development should never be undertaken lightly.

In the following opening moves, White runs into difficulties as a result of a premature attack with Queen and Bishop:

White	Black
1 P—K4	P—K4

So far so good.

2 Q—R5?

This ignores our advice for vigilance when developing major pieces, for the Queen may be driven back by Black, who will attempt to develop *his* pieces in the process. The Queen now attacks the unprotected King's Pawn.

2 ...   Kt—QB3

This develops a minor piece and at the same time protects the King's Pawn. Not 2 ... P—KKt3? for this would allow 3 Q × KP ch. attacking King and Rook, and Black must lose the Rook.

3 B—B4

White may now think he is all set for Scholar's Mate (4 Q × BP).

3 ...   P—KKt3!

This move illustrates the importance of the correct timing of moves, for the advance of this Pawn is now a good move; one move ago it would have been very poor.

4 Q—B3

So White finds he has not been able to checkmate in four moves, but by moving his Queen a second time, hopes to be able to mate next move!

4 ...   Kt—B3

This develops the other Knight to a strong square and at the same time prevents the threatened checkmate.

5 Kt—B3

A good developing move by White at last!

White	Black
5 ...	B—QB4
6 P—Q3	P—Q3
7 Kt—R3	

Not a good square for the Knight; but for the Queen's occupation of the square, the Knight could have occupied KB3.

7 ...	B—KKt5

Instead of threatening checkmate, White now finds his Queen in trouble. *See* Diagram 168.

168

Position after 7 ... B—KKt5

Black has been able to develop all minor pieces to good squares and is able to castle. White, on the other hand, has developed his King's Knight to the side of the board, whilst his Queen's Bishop is still on its starting square. White's further developing moves must be postponed until the harassed Queen is moved to safety.

In the above attempt to give Scholar's Mate, White brought his Queen to the fifth rank on the second move, where it soon became a target. In using up important move time in safeguarding the Queen, Black was able to gain a clear advantage in development, despite the fact that the game is only seven moves old! Black's seventh move is particularly instructive, for it demonstrates the time-saving principle of fulfilling two tasks at once; in this case, the development of the Bishop to a strong square coupled with the further aggravation of the plight of the white Queen.

A repulsed Queen attack in the early part of the game usually results in a decisive loss of move time!

Here are some positions giving examples of strong and weak opening play:

Advantage to White

169

170

White's pieces occupy squares of strength; both Bishops are posted to diagonals where there is freedom of movement, whilst the Knights occupy squares where they enjoy maximum striking power. All four minor pieces hit at the centre, and the King, having been castled King's side, is tucked away to relative safety. Black's position, on the other hand, is cramped; neither Bishop has much freedom of movement. Furthermore, Black has still to castle. In short, *White is in a position to attack now! Black is unready!*

Although Black has developed more wisely than in the previous example, White still has a marked superiority. The awkward position of the black King is the main reason for Black's backwardness in development. Not only does the King separate the Rooks but the King's Rook is completely trapped.

Advantage to Black

171

172

Black has made good progress with sound principles of development in the ideal manner. White, however, is severely restricted on the Queen's side with the Queen's Rook and both Queen's side minor pieces on their starting squares.

Here the positions of White's Bishops mar what is an otherwise reasonable development. The move time spent in advancing the Rooks' Pawns would have been more wisely spent in freeing the Bishops.

Two short games, to end with, to serve as a sombre warning of the dangers of careless mobilisation!

Game 4.

White	Black
1 P—K4	P—K4
2 Kt—KB3	Kt—QB3
3 B—Kt5	P—QR3
4 B—R4	Kt—B3
5 Q—K2	P—QKt4
6 B—Kt3	B—K2
7 P—B3	O—O

See Diagram 173.

Well positioned pieces give good opportunities for winning tactical devices!

173

Position after 7 ... O—O

Both sides have made a good start with their development.

White	Black
8 O—O	P—Q4
9 P×P	Kt×P
10 Kt×P	Kt—B5
11 Q—K4	Kt×Kt

In taking the Knight, Black leaves the Queen's Rook defenceless. White should look carefully at this sacrifice of the exchange of Knight for Rook. Chess players never give up two points for nothing, unless they blunder!

12 Q×R

White decides he may safely take the Rook. *See* Diagram 174.

174

Position after 12 Q×R

White takes the offered Rook, but dangerously slows down his development in the process. Perhaps White, in capturing the Rook, paused to wonder why Black was so generous!

12 ...	Q—Q6
13 B—Q1	

Having been developed to the Queen's side, the Bishop is brought back towards the King's side, which is now being assailed by Black's Queen and two Knights.

White	Black
13 ...	B—KR6

A third minor piece hits at the defences of the white King, at the same time discovering attack against the Queen.

14 Q×P

The Queen remains out of play so far as the critical area of the board is concerned.

14 ...	B×P

Attacking the Rook.

15 R—K1	Q—B6

Black offers up the Queen!

16 B×Q

And White greedily snatches it up!

16 ...	Kt×B mate!

See Diagram 175.

175

Final position after
16 ... Kt×B mate

Black mates with Knight supported by the other Knight and Bishop. It was well worthwhile losing the exchange of Queen's Rook for Knight, in order to draw White's Queen away from the defence of the beleaguered King.

In the final position, White's Queen's Rook and both Queen's side minor pieces are still on their starting squares! White lost valuable developing time in capturing Black's Queen's Rook, which took the capturing piece away from the scene of the onslaught against the white King.

8

Game 5.

	White	Black
1	P—K4	P—K4
2	P—KB4	

A gambit Pawn, offered in order to give White more attacking scope down the King's Bishop's file.

2	...	P×P
3	Kt—KB3	P—KKt4
4	B—B4	P—KB3?

See Diagram 176.

176

Position after 4 ... P—KB3?

Black's last move, in weakening the King's defences, would have been bad even without the white Bishop at B4. In the face of the attack by the Bishop, the move is fatal!

5 Kt×P

A sacrifice which tears a hole in the weakened King's side Pawn defences, and clears the way for the white Queen.

5	...	P×Kt
6	Q—R5 ch	K—K2
7	Q—B7 ch	K—Q3
8	Q—Q5 ch	K—K2
9	Q—K5 mate	

See Diagram 177.

177

Position after 9 Q—K5 mate

White developed his Queen and two minor pieces. All three pieces were used in the attack against the black King.

Not many games come to such a rapid end, and in order to checkmate in nine moves in this way, the loser has to co-operate, to some extent, in his own downfall!

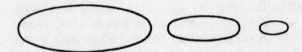

'Had that game in the palm of my hand—and blundered! Had a move that would have won with ease, but was so put off by his surprise attack that it completely slipped my mind. . . . My approach is much too haphazard. . . . Must get some kind of "drill" to follow when it's my turn to move. . . .'

CHAPTER 12

THE ADVANTAGE OF THE INITIATIVE

We commenced this book with an explanation of the battlefield and the forces to be engaged. We conclude with consideration of an element which often brings victory in its wake—the initiative!

A player who enjoys an advantage in either material or development, or both, is in the happy position of being able not only to exploit his advantage but also to choose the time, place and method of the exploitation! A player who is losing in the development race, must be prepared to find himself at the receiving end of an attack, the timing and direction of which are naturally unannounced. Just as a boxer may reel under one blow, only to suffer another before he has time to recover his balance, so a chess player may be faced with a series of hammer blows across the board. The initiative created in either case is often the prelude to defeat.

Since the initiative is the natural outcome of sound mobilisation, little advantage is to be gained by attacking before development is complete; in fact, time wasted by premature attack, is, as we have seen, a common cause of defeat. The player, however, who is first in a position to launch an attack from strength, is well on the way to victory.

So far as attack and defence are concerned, the best outlook for a chess player to adopt is one which safeguards equally the needs of both features. If, however, you *must* be labelled either as a defensive or an attacking player, be an attacking player. You will win more games this way than you will by persistently being on the defensive!

Criticism of poor moves illustrated in this book must never be taken as a recommendation for over-caution. A good chess player has adventurous and fighting qualities, which encourage him to seek out, and rapidly exploit, enemy weaknesses. You should experiment with every kind of short cut to victory, including methods we have warned against! The principles we have recommended will serve you much better if you prove their value by experience, than if you merely take them as read!

Mobilise rapidly, then attack, attack, attack!

CHAPTER 13

MOVE DRILL

It's my turn to move . . .

Does his last move threaten me . . .?
Shall I postpone my planned move to deal with his threat . . .
or is my idea strong enough to go forward . . .?

I've made up my mind . . . just before I move, though . . .

Eyes twice round the board:

1. To see if I can find a better move still!
2. To make sure I haven't made an oversight!

Drill complete . . . so here goes . . .

DO YOU KNOW . . .

. . . **what a chess clock is?** A chess clock is really a pair of clocks with stop watch actions, which are so connected that when one clock is started, the other stops (*see* Plate 3). When White has made his first move, he presses a switch which not only stops *his* clock, but starts his opponent's clock at the same time. Thus one clockface records the time taken for the moves of the player with the white pieces, the other recording his opponent's move time. When using a chess clock you are required to make a given number of moves (or more) in a stated time. A player who fails to make the requisite number of moves in the specified time forfeits the game.

. . . **about the British Chess Federation?** The B.C.F., as it is usually known, controls nearly all organised chess in the United Kingdom. Counties are affiliated to one or other of the large chess Unions, which are, themselves, affiliated, together with a number of non-territorial organisations, to the Federation. The B.C.F. is responsible for the championships which produce the British Champion each year. Information about affiliated organisations and many other matters of interest, may be found in the British Chess Federation Year Book, which is published from time to time and obtainable from the Hon. Secretary of the Federation at its registered address: 9A Grand Parade, St. Leonards-on-Sea, Sussex.

. . . **about the International Chess Federation?** The International Chess Federation (Fédération Internationale des Echecs—'F.I.D.E.') organises the world individual and team championships, and its authority extends to all parts of the world. F.I.D.E. also regulates and interprets the rules of the game.

. . . **how to find the address of your nearest chess club?** Your local library will probably have the name and address of your local chess club secretary in its directory. Should the library not be able to help, however, you should write to the Hon. Secretary of the British Chess Federation, at the address given above, enclosing a stamped, addressed envelope.

. . . about etiquette and good manners in chess? It is courteous to avoid any kind of behaviour which may distract your opponent when it is his turn to move. Never indulge in conversation with friends who may be watching the game, whilst your opponent is thinking out his move. If you wish to talk in such circumstances, move away from the board. It would be unfair to receive helpful advice on the game in progress, during such discussions! [Never touch a piece and then change your mind about moving it, if it is your turn to move. Apart from being poor etiquette, it is against the rules of the game to touch a piece which may legally be moved, then set it down and move another piece after a change of heart.] Finally, don't be a 'hand hoverer'! Avoid reaching out to make a move, then drawing back, then reaching out again, in a state of uncertainty. Keep your hands right away from the board until you have made up your mind and completed your move 'drill'. And when you do move, do it deliberately—and hope for the best!

. . . how to record the position of an unfinished game in Forsyth Notation? This form of recording is invaluable when it is not possible to keep an unfinished game set up on the chessboard. This is how it works. Commence recording Black's first rank pieces, starting with square QR1. To distinguish black pieces from white, we put rings round the black pieces. We will record the position shown in Diagram 178:

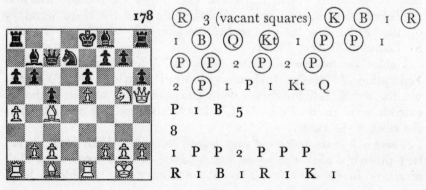

178   (R)   3 (vacant squares)   (K) (B)   1   (R)
  1   (B)   (Q)   (Kt)   1   (P)   (P)   1
  (P)   (P)   2   (P)   2   (P)
  2   (P)   1   P   1   Kt   Q
  P   1   B   5
  8
  1   P   P   2   P   P   P
  R   1   B   1   R   1   K   1

To save space, the notation may be given along the line, with a comma between each rank, i.e.:

Ⓡ 3 Ⓚ Ⓑ 1 Ⓡ, 1 Ⓑ Ⓠ Ⓚt 1 Ⓟ Ⓟ 1, Ⓟ Ⓟ 2 Ⓟ 2 Ⓟ,
2 Ⓟ 1 P 1 Kt Q, P 1 B 5, 8, 1 P P 2 P P P, R 1 B 1 R 1 K 1.

. . . **the traditional method used to determine who is to play with the white pieces, in friendly games?** Either player takes one Pawn of each colour and shuffles them in the hands behind his back. He then holds his fists forward, one Pawn hidden in each. His opponent takes his pick, and plays with the colour of the Pawn he selects.

. . . **what a travelling set is?** There are many excellent miniature chess sets on the market (*see* Plate 5), including wallet sets which fold up as slim as pocket-diaries, which are very useful when playing games away from home or for recording positions. These sets are not, however, good substitutes for full-sized boards and sets for serious and regular play. Travelling sets have the advantage, not only of fitting the pocket, but in being able to be closed up mid-way through a game. It is well-nigh impossible, however, to give full scope to the spacial concepts of the game, when only a few inches separate one end of the board from the other!

. . **the** *British Chess Magazine*, **or the magazine** *Chess*? Both magazines include games, chess problems, news items, announcements concerning annual or special tournaments, etc. The publishers also sell books in many languages on all aspects of the game, boards, sets, chess clocks, score sheets, scorebooks and every other kind of chess material. Best of all are the correspondence columns, in which you can air grievances, sing praises or crave assistance! Here are the addresses of the two magazines:

British Chess Magazine, 9 Market Street, St. Leonards-on-Sea, Sussex.
Chess, Sutton Coldfield.

Appendix II

GLOSSARY OF CHESS TERMS

This appendix contains not only chess terms found earlier in this book, but others which you may come across in other chess books and periodicals.

Algebraic notation	A system of notation used in many parts of the world.
Back row	The first rank of either side of the board.
Blindfold chess	Where one or both opponents make the moves without sight of the board. In cases where both opponents play blindfold (no actual blindfold is used) a referee usually plays the moves on a board at the instruction of the opponents.
Check	When the King is attacked.
Checkmate	When a King cannot escape check.
Combination	A series of forced moves.
Correspondence chess	Where the moves are recorded on a score-sheet, and exchanged by correspondence, between opponents who are unable to meet across the board.
Defend	To protect or support a piece against possible or actual attack.
Descriptive notation	The system of notation used in this book.
Development	The action of bringing pieces on to squares in readiness for attack or defence.
Diagonals	The slanting rows of squares, as illustrated on page 16 (Diagrams 6 and 7).
Discovered attack	A position in which one piece has been removed to uncover an attack by another.
Discovered check	A position in which a piece has been moved to uncover check.

Double attack	Two pieces attacked at the same time.
Double check	A position in which the King is in check from two pieces at the same time.
Doubled Pawns	Pawns of the same colour standing on the same file.
En passant	A special kind of Pawn capturing move ('in passing').
En prise	A piece is said to be *en prise* when it is under attack.
Escape square	A square to which an attacked piece, usually a King, may go.
Exchange	A series of moves in which each side captures pieces.
Exposed	When a piece, usually a King, is without shelter from possible attack.
Files	Lines of squares running directly across the board from a player's nearside to the farside. *See* page 16 (Diagram 5).
Flight square	An escape square.
Forced move	No other move possible.
Fork	An attack against two or more pieces at the same time.
Gambit	An opening where a Pawn or piece is sacrificed, with the intention of gaining an advantage in development.
Illegal	Not allowed by the rules of the game.
Interpose	To move a piece in between an attacked piece and its attacker.
Isolated Pawn	One which has no Pawn of the same colour on either adjoining file.
J'adoube	'I adjust'. A warning given when a player wishes to adjust a piece on its square.
Lightning chess	An event where moves are made every five or ten seconds upon the sounding of a buzzer or bell signal, given at appropriate intervals.
Lines	Ranks, files or diagonals.
Major piece	Queen or Rook.

Master	National chess title awarded to selected players who have achieved a particularly high standard in competitive play at an advanced level. The title International Master is awarded by the International Chess Federation, who also award the premier title, Grandmaster.
Minor piece	Bishop or Knight.
Mobile	Able to move freely.
Open file	A file on which there are no Pawns.
Opening	The commencing moves of a game.
Passed Pawn	A Pawn which has no opponent's Pawn in front of it on its own file, and which, in advancing to the eighth rank, does not have to pass an opponent's Pawn on either of the adjoining files.
Perpetual check	Where a player may check non-stop.
Pin	When a piece is unable to move from its line without exposing another piece to attack.
Position	The arrangement of the pieces during the course of a game.
Promotion	When a Pawn, in reaching the eighth rank, must be changed to any other piece of the same colour, except a King.
Queening	When a Pawn is promoted to Queen.
Ranks	Lines of squares running across the board from left to right, as illustrated on page 16 (Diagram 4).
Sacrifice	Giving up a piece in order to gain an advantage.
Simultaneous display	An event in which one player plays a number of opponents at the same time, where the principal player makes a move on each board in turn. (*See* Plate 7.)
Skewer	An attack upon two pieces on the same line, where the piece nearest the attacker is compelled to move, leaving the other to be captured.
Smothered mate	Checkmate by a Knight, where all the escape squares of the attacked King are occupied by other pieces. *See* page 55 (Diagram 76).

Stalemate   A drawn position where a player is not in check but is unable to move.

Trapped   No escape.

Under-promotion   Promotion of a Pawn to Rook, Knight or Bishop.

Wing   The right- or left-hand side of the board.

Appendix III

SOLUTIONS

SOLUTIONS TO TEST 1

Q.1. There are forty-two straight lines of squares on the chessboard, made up of eight ranks, eight files and twenty-six diagonals. The shortest diagonals are two squares long, whilst the longest are eight squares long (page 16 refers).

Q.2. There are eighteen straight lines of eight squares on the chessboard, eight ranks, eight files and two diagonals. (There is one long diagonal of eight black squares and one of eight white squares) (page 16 refers).
Note. There is no great merit in remembering exactly how many rows of squares there are on the chessboard, but if you have been surprised at the number of straight paths there are, you will have learned a useful lesson concerning the many lines along which the rival forces will travel.

Q.3. No, there is no way of avoiding the re-arrangement of pieces, if the board has been set up the wrong way round. Experiment, if you remain unconvinced! (page 14 refers).

Q.4. All pieces in their starting positions, face their opposite numbers at the other end of the files (page 14 refers).

Q.5. If you are White, the Queen's side of the board is on the left (page 14 refers).

Q.6. No penalty may be exacted if a player adjusts a piece without prior warning, if it is his opponent's turn to move (page 15 refers).

Q.7. The ranks and files referred to, are indicated in Diagram 179. Note that White's second rank is the same as Black's seventh rank (pages 18 and 19 refer).

Q.8. The squares marked ϕ in Diagram 10 are identified by the appropriate square numbers in Diagram 180. To avoid confusion, the black square numbers are shown in reverse (page 19 refers).

179

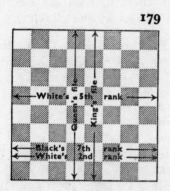

180

SOLUTIONS TO TEST 2

181

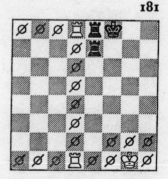

Q.1. The vacant squares attacked by the white pieces are shown marked ϕ in Diagram 181. In addition, the Rook at Black's K1 is attacked (pages 22–24 refer).

Q.2. The white Rook at KKt7 may be captured by either of Black's Rooks. Since this white Rook is protected by the other Rook, it would be illegal for Black's King to effect the capture, for a player may not put himself into check (pages 22–27 refer).

Q.3. White is in check, so the only possible move is the capture by the King of the Rook at Black's QR8. Note that White's QR2, QKt2 and QB1 are under attack and therefore 'out of bounds' to the white King. Moreover, the white King may not capture the Rook at Black's QB7, for this is protected by the black King (pages 22–27 refer).

Q.4. It is clear that it is White to move because White is in check. A player may never legally be in check and yet not have the next move, unless it is checkmate! (pages 25 and 26 refer).

Q.5. After White has captured the Rook on Black's QR8, Black follows by playing the remaining Rook to QB8 checkmate! (pages 26 and 27 refer).

Q.6. In the position shown in Diagram 182 White may give checkmate with a white Rook placed on any of the squares marked × and a white King on White's Q6. Although a Rook at White's Q7 would give check, it would not be checkmate, for Black's King would be able to escape to either QB1 or K1 (pages 26 and 27 refer).

182

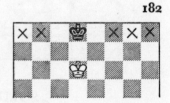

SOLUTIONS TO TEST 3

Q.1. A Bishop may, in due course, attack or occupy half the total number of squares of the chessboard—thirty-two squares. A black square Bishop may attack thirty-two black squares; the white square Bishop thirty-two white squares (page 29 refers).

Q.2. (i) A Queen, moving along all ranks, files and diagonals, is able to attack or occupy every square of the chessboard.
(ii) A Knight may also, in due course, attack or occupy every square of the chessboard (pages 30–32 refer).

Q.3. The Queen, in attacking twenty-seven squares, is the most powerful piece. The maximum square attacking power of the other pieces is shown below:

Rook . 14 squares
Bishop . 13 squares
Knight . 8 squares

(pages 22, 23, and 29–32 refer).

Q.4. The maximum number of squares which may be attacked by a Pawn is two (pages 35–36 refer).

Q.5. The Rook, in attacking fourteen squares from any square on an otherwise empty chessboard, does not increase its square attacking power the nearer it gets to the centre of the chessboard (page 23 refers).

Q.6. (Diagram 49). A black Queen may give checkmate from Black's QB8.
(Diagram 50). A black Knight may give checkmate from either Black's QKt6 or QB7.
(Diagram 51). The black square Bishop may give checkmate from Black's QB6. Square QKt7 would be of no use, of course, for the King would simply capture it.
(Diagram 52). Black may give checkmate next move, by capturing the white Rook and being promoted to either Queen or Rook. The promoted Pawn would be free from capture by the white King, because of the protection afforded by the Bishop at Q5 (pages 26–27 refer).

Q.7. Capture *en passant* is not possible here, for although the Pawn has moved to the side of the black Pawn on the adjacent file, it is not the white Pawn's *first* move (page 36 refers).

Q.8. The only Pawn able to move is the black Pawn on K6. The only move this Pawn may make is to capture the Knight. Like the other Pawns, the black Pawn on K6 may not advance along its file, since it is blocked (pages 33 and 35 refer).

Q.9. Black may castle in this position, for there is no objection to putting your opponent in check, in the act of castling (pages 37–39 refer).

9

Q.10. The King should be moved first, when castling. Failure to do this may result in your opponent insisting that the move be a Rook move only (page 38 refers).

SOLUTIONS TO TEST 4

Q.1. Here is the position at the conclusion of the exchanges referred to:

183

Judged solely by the table of relative values, after 1 Kt × P, R × Kt; 2 B × R, K × B; both sides have given up the equivalent of six points and from the arithmetical point of view the exchange is equal. There are two more aspects to be borne in mind, however. First, White has exchanged two usefully developed minor pieces *which have used up five moves*; the Rook and Pawn which Black has given up, on the other hand, have used three moves between them. Second, whereas White has exchanged two *active* minor pieces, Black has given up a previously unmoved Pawn and a Rook which was not yet in active play. White has really given away two moves. If you should think two wasted moves to be unimportant, try giving an opponent of equivalent playing strength, a two-move start in a game! The exchange is, therefore, in Black's favour (page 43 refers).

Q.2. Black's Pawn should be promoted to a Rook. Black may then force checkmate in four more moves (see if you can find out how). If the promotion is to a Queen, Black's advantage is wasted, for White is stalemated. Black would still win in the end, if the promotion were to a minor piece or even if the Pawn concerned were not promoted at all. The quickest way of winning is always the best, however, and promotion to Rook is the right answer (page 57 refers).

Q.3. The two Rooks in Diagram 82 are superior to the Queen in Diagram 83, for the two Rooks are immediately able to capture the Pawn without loss, whereas the Queen, unable to make a safe capture unaided, must wait to bring up the King in support (page 43 refers).

Q.4. Here is the final position you should have reached:

184

Black is checkmated (pages 45–49 refer).

Q.5. White forces a draw by R—QR3 ch. and after ... K or P×R, White is unable to move and yet is not in check—stalemate (pages 57 and 58 refer).

Q.6. (Diagram 85). White Rook checkmates on QB1, Q1, K1, KB1, KKt1 or KR1.
(Diagram 86). Black Queen checkmates on QKt7.
(Diagram 87). Black Knight checkmates on QB7.
(Diagram 88). White Rook checkmates on QB8, Q8, K8, KB8, KKt8 or KR8.
(Diagram 89). Black Queen checkmates on either QR7 or QB8.
(Diagram 90). A black Rook checkmates on QB8, Q8, K8, KB8, KKt8 or KR8 (pages 51–55 refer).

SOLUTIONS TO TEST 5

Q.1. The white King must move up the board to his Pawns, and shepherd one or both to queen. In the meantime the black King must ply helplessly between B1 and Kt2, for he may not capture the Pawn on White's Kt6 without allowing the other Pawn to queen (page 65 refers).

Q.2. Without outside support, and assuming best play, it is not possible for either side to force a passed Pawn. For example:

1 P—R5	P×P
2 P×P	

and the position is blocked.

If 1 ... P—Kt4, we have another blocked position.

It is, however, possible to force a passed Pawn in the case of two rows of three or more Pawns facing each other, as described in Diagram 98 (page 67 refers).

Q.3.   1 K—B5

Since it is now Black's turn to move, we can implement the counting rule. The Pawn has four moves to reach its queening square, the same number of moves as it would take the white King. Since the Pawn is unable to reach its queening square in fewer moves than the opposing King, the Pawn will be captured. The game will thus be drawn (page 68 refers).

Q.4. Since the shepherding King is *behind* the advancing Pawn, instead of in front of it, Black will be able to prevent the Pawn from queening, e.g.:

1 ...	K—K2
2 K—Q5	

Now the black King should face the white King.

2 ...	K—Q2
3 P—K6 ch	K—K2
4 K—K5	K—K1
5 K—Q6	K—Q1

The facing position once more.

6 P—K7 ch	K—K1

And now the white King either moves to K6 stalemate, or deserts the Pawn. The game will be drawn.

If White plays 2 K—B5, instead of 2 K—Q5, a similar pattern of events arises, again resulting in a draw. Play through alternative variations for yourself (pages 69–72 refer).

Q.5.   1 ...   K—K1

Into the facing position.

                        2 P—Q7 ch   K—Q1

And White stalemates, or deserts the Pawn (pages 69–72 refer).

Q.6.   1 P—Q7   K—B2
                        2 K—K7

And White will queen the Pawn next move (pages 69–72 refer).

Q.7.   (i) White to play. The white King must retreat, Black having the
        opposition.

                        1 K—K4   K—B3
                        2 K—B4   K—K2 or Kt2

To retain the opposition it is necessary for the King concerned
to move into the facing position, thus forcing the other King to give
ground. It is for this reason that Black moves the King to K2,
for if, instead, 2 ... K—B2, then 3 K—B5 gives White the
opposition.

                        3 K—B5   K—B2

We are back to where we started, still with White to move.
Work out the variation which would follow from 1 K—Kt4.
With White to play, therefore, a draw results.
(ii) Black to play. White has the opposition.

                        1 ...   K—K2
                        2 K—Kt6

White will now capture the black Pawn on KR3. If Black
blocks the queening of the white Pawn on R5, the white King
will move over to capture the other black Pawn. Since the black
King cannot be in two places at once, one of the white Pawns
will queen, giving White an easy win.
If 1 ... K—Kt2; 2 K—K6, K—B1; 3 K×P, K—K1; 4 K—B7,
White will queen the Pawn (pages 69–72 refer).

Q.8. Black wins with:

| 1 ... | R—QB1 ch |
| 2 K—Kt1, 2 or 3 | K×R |

(pages 73–75 refer).

Q.9. 1 Kt—Kt4!

Attacking Black's Knight. If now:

| 1 ... | Kt×Kt |
| 2 P—Kt8 = Q | |

And White has an easy win (pages 76 and 77 refer).

Q.10. 1 ... P—B7!

If now 2 Q—Kt3 ch., K—R8; 3 Q×P stalemate. With careful play, Black may thus force a draw, for the threat of queening the Pawn gives White no time to bring his King to assist in the attack (pages 77 and 78 refer).

SOLUTIONS TO TEST 6

Q.1.

1 R×P ch	K—Kt1
2 R—R8 ch	K×R
3 Q—R6 ch	K—Kt1
4 Q—Kt7 mate	

If 1 ... P×R; 2 Q—Kt5 (attacking the black Pawn at KR4 and threatening Q—Kt7 mate). 2 ... R—KKt1 is no defence to 2 Q—Kt5, for White then mates with 3 Q×RP.

This is another example of the sacrifice of material in order to force an advantage, in this case, checkmate.

Q.2. The white Bishop at K2, which is pinned, is attacked by Black's Queen and Rook and defended by Queen (QR6) and King.

1 ... B—Kt4!

This blocks the defensive action of the white Queen. Note that 2 P×B would still leave the line blocked. Since White is now threatened with ... Q×B mate, Black must give up the Queen and devote his immediate attention to protecting the King by Kt—K3.

Q.3.   1 Q×RP ch   K×Q
          2 P×P double checkmate!

Remember that in all cases of double check, the attacked King
must move, in order to relieve the check. Since, in this case, the
attacked King is unable to move, it is checkmate. White ably
demonstrates here that there is something more valuable than
even a Queen—checkmate!

Q.4.   1 ...   R×KtP ch

Discovering attack against the white Queen. Since White must
get out of check next move, he has no time to save the Queen.

Q.5. A stronger move than the capture of the black Rook on K2
exists!

          1 Either Kt×KBP ch   P×Kt
          2 The other Kt×P ch

And Black's King and Queen are forked. After the King moves
out of check, White follows with 3 Kt×Q.

Q.6.   1 B—QKt5

Pinning the white Queen against the King.

          1 ...   P×B
          2 P×P

Attacking Queen with the Pawn and at the same time uncovering
attack on Black's Queen's Rook by White's opposite number.
In salvaging the Queen, Black must give up the Rook, and White
benefits from the exchange.

(Pages 83–95 refer.)

DIAGRAM
REFERENCE
PAGE

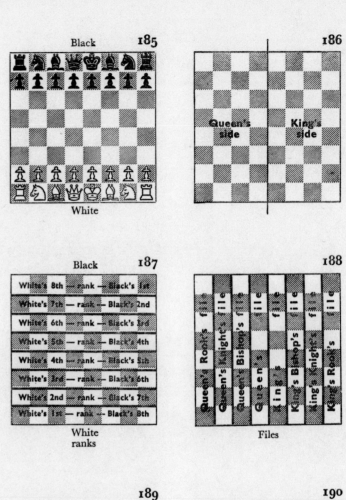

Black 185

White

186

Queen's side   King's side

Black 187

White ranks

White's 8th — rank — Black's 1st
White's 7th — rank — Black's 2nd
White's 6th — rank — Black's 3rd
White's 5th — rank — Black's 4th
White's 4th — rank — Black's 5th
White's 3rd — rank — Black's 6th
White's 2nd — rank — Black's 7th
White's 1st — rank — Black's 8th

188

Files

Queen's Rook's file
Queen's Knight's file
Queen's Bishop's file
Queen's file
King's file
King's Bishop's file
King's Knight's file
King's Rook's file

189

QR8	QKt8	QB8	Q8	K8	KB8	KKt8	KR8
QR7	QKt7	QB7	Q7	K7	KB7	KKt7	KR7
QR6	QKt6	QB6	Q6	K6	KB6	KKt6	KR6
QR5	QKt5	QB5	Q5	K5	KB5	KKt5	KR5
QR4	QKt4	QB4	Q4	K4	KB4	KKt4	KR4
QR3	QKt3	QB3	Q3	K3	KB3	KKt3	KR3
QR2	QKt2	QB2	Q2	K2	KB2	KKt2	KR2
QR1	QKt1	QB1	Q1	K1	KB1	KKt1	KR1

Square labels for
WHITE pieces

190

QR1	QKt1	QB1	Q1	K1	KB1	KKt1	KR1
QR2	QKt2	QB2	Q2	K2	KB2	KKt2	KR2
QR3	QKt3	QB3	Q3	K3	KB3	KKt3	KR3
QR4	QKt4	QB4	Q4	K4	KB4	KKt4	KR4
QR5	QKt5	QB5	Q5	K5	KB5	KKt5	KR5
QR6	QKt6	QB6	Q6	K6	KB6	KKt6	KR6
QR7	QKt7	QB7	Q7	K7	KB7	KKt7	KR7
QR8	QKt8	QB8	Q8	K8	KB8	KKt8	KR8

Square labels for
BLACK pieces

INDEX